101
ways
to find
calm

How to use your body
to soothe your mind

Rebekah Ballagh

ALLEN&UNWIN
SYDNEY•MELBOURNE•AUCKLAND•LONDON

First published in 2024

Text and illustrations © Rebekah Ballagh, 2024

Allen & Unwin
Level 2, 10 College Hill, Freemans Bay
Auckland 1011, New Zealand
Phone: (64 9) 377 3800
Email: auckland@allenandunwin.com
Web: www.allenandunwin.co.nz

83 Alexander Street
Crows Nest NSW 2065, Australia
Phone: (61 2) 8425 0100

A catalogue record for this book is available from
the National Library of New Zealand.

ISBN 978 1 99100 603 5

Design by Kate Barraclough
Author photograph by Tessa Jaine
Set in Untitled Sans, Quotes and Texts and Dreaming Outloud
Printed in China by 1010 Printing Ltd

10 9 8 7 6 5 4 3 2 1

MIX
Paper | Supporting
responsible forestry
FSC
www.fsc.org
FSC® C016973

 # CONTENTS

INTRODUCTION

Many people feel like their body isn't peaceful to live in and their lives are a source of overwhelming triggers and trials.

It doesn't have to be this way.

I invite you to go through the pages of this book with an open heart and mind; experimenting and practising with compassion, grace and non-judgemental acceptance.

You can create a toolkit of powerful practices that will return you to calm during times of stress, and set a new baseline of regulation and resilience in your everyday life.

I believe that all humans are born with an innate capacity for healing. Inevitably, you may face challenges in your life that cloud your journey. Perhaps at times you feel hypervigilant and armoured for self-protection, and other times you feel disconnected and shut down for self-preservation.

Whether you are actively working through chronic patterns of stress, anxiety, trauma and low mood or just wanting to deepen your practice of peace and connection to self, this book has you covered.

Each page provides you with a powerful tool for calm and connection. Practices are bite-sized and simple to read but they can make a world of difference.

The practices combine a range of scientifically backed methods, with influences from mindfulness, meditation and somatic therapies, polyvagal exercises, yin yoga and EMDR (Eye Movement Desensitization and Reprocessing). The 'Useful terms' section at the end of the book explains some of the technical terms you'll find throughout the book.

You'll learn how to come home to your body, to deeply connect with yourself, to safely feel and process your emotions and to rewire your brain and nervous system. You'll experience a wonderful connection with your body as you deepen your ability for compassion, presence and healing.

HOW TO USE THIS BOOK

Let's start with the foundations: compassion, acceptance, non-judgement, mindful observation and presence.

I encourage you to bring an attitude of curiosity, playfulness even, and an openness and patience to just 'be' with whatever comes up.

Sometimes body (somatic) and mindfulness practices will create the space for tricky feelings to come to the forefront. These practices can release emotions and trauma in the body so you may experience feelings of grief, sadness or anger as you work through some of the tools in this book. You'll likely also experience deep relaxation, relief, presence and ease.

Here's the key: if you are able to simply 'be' with any tricky emotions that arise and if you feel steady (regulated) enough to 'hold mindfulness' (non-judgement, presence, compassion), then stay with the process. However, if you notice yourself becoming dysregulated or feeling hijacked by big emotions or a threat response (overwhelming anxiety, dissociation), this is a sign that you're not quite ready for the practice and don't have the capacity in that moment. That is absolutely okay. Come out of the practice, walk around, have a drink of water and debrief with a trusted friend or a professional.

Trust your body and its healing process. If something feels too much, then gently slow down.

During your practices you may notice signs of release, which means your nervous system is settling and emotions are flowing again. These signs include deep sighs, yawns, spontaneous swallows, tummy gurgles and emotional releases like crying, laughing or a feeling of settling and deep relaxation.

Stick with it. Practice makes progress. In order to rewire your brain and nervous system you need to practise these tools not just when you are distressed but when you are calm too, creating pathways in your brain that you can use when you're feeling tripped up. I always say: *practise in the calm to access in the chaos.* You may have had years of reacting (often unconsciously) in a certain way to stress, so allow yourself space and grace.

When I guide clients through these practices I go slowly, taking my time with cues that encourage self-connection and presence. In the interests of keeping the practices in this book easy to read and understand, I have removed a lot of this extra cueing. For this reason I encourage you to have the following prompts in mind for most of the practices ahead.

These little touchstones will help you to get the most out of each practice:

🌸 Keep coming back to your breath. Notice how you are breathing, notice the air entering your nostrils and lungs, your belly expanding. Slow your exhales. If your mind wanders, come back to this anchor.

🌸 Slow down and practise presence. Try not to just 'go through the motions'. Really feel it. Notice the way your body moves, your breath feels and your mind behaves.

❀ Observe any habitual body patterns. Notice if your shoulders are hunched, if your jaw is tight or your teeth clenched. Check for bracing through your stomach, clenching in your eyes or tightness in your body. Simply witness and reset.

❀ Where appropriate, allow your muscles and mind to settle. Release resistance, bracing and tension. Picture things slowing, melting, sinking, becoming heavy and calm.

❀ Be a witness to your thoughts and emotions as you hold curiosity, non-judgement and compassion towards them. You are not your thoughts. You are not your emotions.

When using this book, feel free to dip in and out of the practices in any order you like. You don't need to follow their order in this book. If you're unsure how to choose a tool or which tools work to support specific emotions or struggles, you might like to turn to the 'Ideas for Daily Practice' section at the back of this book for guidance and examples of tools to try.

The beauty of this book is that the tools are accessible, digestible, simple and brief — flip open a page and experiment!

Many of the tools are interchangeable; they work well across a range of emotions.

It's useful to have an open mind and try each and every tool in this book. Come back and try again if a tool feels challenging or 'doesn't work' for you the first time. The key is repetition and an open, curious mind. See the back of the book for an explanation of complex terms.

Finally, try to incorporate at least one tool into each and every day.

BEFORE AND AFTER

Checking in with yourself before and after using
any tool in this book will help you to tune into
your emotions and provide you with feedback
about any shifts that have happened.

Before using a tool, ask yourself:

🌸 How am I feeling? Can I name any emotions I am experiencing right now?

🌸 What is happening in my body? Where do I feel those emotions in my body? What sensations am I aware of physically?

🌸 What are my thoughts doing right now? Do I notice any particular thoughts? Are my thoughts racing, sluggish, spacey or jumbled?

🌸 What would I score my overall level of discomfort or distress out of ten right now?

Then go ahead with your practice. Afterwards, check in using the same questions.

Do not label the outcome as good or bad. You are providing feedback and a mind—body connection; you don't have to get rid of a feeling. This is about non-judgemental observation without attachment to the outcome.

MAKE SOME
CHOICES TODAY THAT
FUTURE YOU WILL LOOK
BACK ON AND SAY
'THANK YOU!'

1

FOCUS SWINGING

This powerful practice allows your nervous system to process emotions and distress.

You'll learn to sit with tricky experiences and then find your way back to calm.

Here's how:

1. Begin by intentionally creating some discomfort in your body by coming into a position like a toe sit (see illustration), or anything else that feels a little uncomfortable.

2. Notice any physical sensations, resistance and thoughts that arise. Stay with this for 30–60 seconds.

3. Swing your focus to an area of your body that feels safe or neutral. Gently move this part of your body. Stay with this for 30–60 seconds.

4. Move your focus back and forward between these two states a few times. Finish by sitting comfortably and reflecting on your experience.

When you are ready, you can try this with an emotion or a tricky thought. Mindfully sit and observe the distress (without judgement or resistance) then swing your focus to a tool that helps you feel calm (like #27 or #97).

2

SENSORY GROUNDING

Do you ever find yourself on autopilot, going through the motions of your day without being fully present? You can create micro mindful moments of calm and regulation for your nervous system by practising sensory grounding throughout your day.

Here are five ways to do this using each of your senses:

- 🌸 **SiGHT:** Look around and notice three green things, then three patterns, then three things with circles on them.

- 🌸 **HEARiNG:** Close your eyes and list all the sounds you hear.

- 🌸 **TOUCH:** Connect to three things you can feel in your body or touch three things around you.

- 🌸 **SMELL:** Notice any smells or move around and find three things to smell.

- 🌸 **TASTE:** See if you can pick up any lingering tastes in your mouth. You can also find something to eat and take a slow and mindful first bite, describing the flavours to yourself.

3

5-4-3-2-1

This tool helps you settle your mind
with a 'countdown to calm'.

Here's how; notice:

❀ five things you can see (look for interesting
textures, tiny details or patterns of light or
colour)

❀ four things you can feel (notice physical
sensations or move about your space and
touch four different things)

❀ three things you can hear

❀ two things you can smell

❀ one thing you can taste.

DROP YOUR ARMOUR

Isometric muscle relaxation teaches you the difference between tension and relaxation — try this when you're feeling stressed or anxious.

Hold each muscle group tense for 7 seconds then release, allowing it to feel heavy. Visualise tension melting away like honey. It's useful to say a cue to yourself when you relax your muscles like 'Let go', 'Soften' or 'Relax'.

Areas to tense:

- Hold on to the bottom of your seat and pull yourself down into it, feeling tension in your arms and shoulders.

- Scrunch up all your face muscles.

- Tense through your chest and belly, like you're bracing to be tackled.

- Squeeze your glutes together.

- Flex your feet and tense all the muscles in your legs.

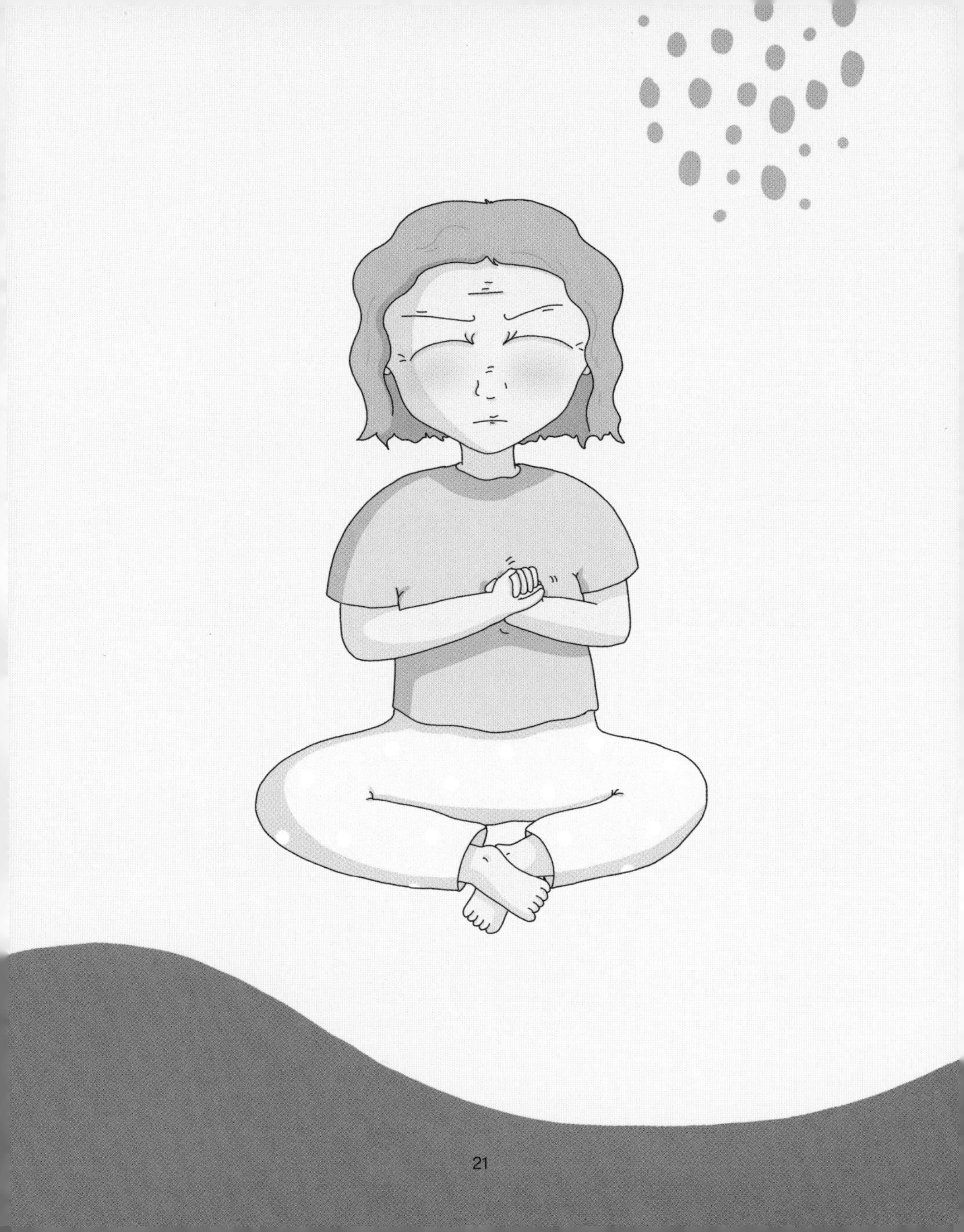

5

FULL BODY RELAXATION

This progressive muscle relaxation practice
is the perfect way to relax your whole body
and send you off to sleep. Try it in bed!

Here's how:

1. Lie down somewhere comfortable and close your eyes.

2. Move through each area of your body, starting at your feet, tensing and squeezing each muscle group. Hold the tension for 7 seconds then release and completely relax.

3. Notice how each area feels after releasing tension. Does it feel heavy, relaxed and grounded?

4. Move through this sequence: feet → calves → thighs → glutes → stomach → chest → arms → shoulders → back (draw your shoulder blades together) → neck (look up) → jaw (open mouth wide) → eyes (squeeze tightly shut).

6

FOCUS SWITCHING

This powerful practice trains your ability to switch your focus and discover which type of mindful focal point works best for you.

Here's how:

1. Notice a niggle or pain in your body or an uncomfortable emotion you are experiencing, or practise by creating some physical discomfort in your body (such as a toe sit).

2. Focus on the feeling of discomfort. Notice thoughts, emotions and sensations. Allow yourself to place judgements; perhaps thinking 'I don't like this feeling' or 'I want this to be over'. This mirrors the way we often respond to discomfort in life. Stay here for 30–60 seconds.

3. Switch your focus to compassion. Continue to feel the discomfort, only now breathe into it. Imagine your inhale wrapping the discomfort with love. Repeat to yourself 'I allow this feeling to be here', 'This will pass' or 'I send love and kindness to this sensation'. Stay here for 30–60 seconds.

4. Switch your focus to an area in your body that feels safe and neutral. Pour all your attention into this place, noticing how it feels and gently moving this area. Stay here for 30–60 seconds.

5. Switch your focus to the external world. Look around the space you are in and notice objects, colours, textures and light. Tune in to the sounds around you. Stay here for 30–60 seconds.

6. Get comfortable and take some time to reflect. Which focus point was the most uncomfortable? Which gave you the most peace?

Begin to practise switching your focus with tricky emotions, memories or thoughts that come up in your day-to-day life.

7

MINDFUL CUP OF TEA

Here is a lovely little mindful moment
you can weave into every day.

Here's how:

1. Sit somewhere cosy with a cuppa.

2. Witness your body: the feeling of your back against your seat; your feet on the floor; the weight of the cup of tea and the feeling of the hot mug warming your hands.

3. Take a long slow inhale, savouring the drink's aroma.

4. Observe all the visual details of your tea, noticing the way the light is bouncing off the liquid, the colour, the texture of the mug and so on.

5. Finally, take a sip. Feel the heat on your tongue, embrace the flavour and the way it feels as you swallow.

POSTURAL SHIFTS

The state of your nervous system affects your posture.

When you are in a sympathetic nervous system state (anxious or angry) you may feel tense & on-guard. When you are in your dorsal vagal state (feeling low or stuck) you may collapse inward, drooping and slumping.

Some examples of postures you take on when:

🌼 *ANXIOUS:* raised shoulders, tight chest, tense stomach

🌼 *ANGRY:* clenched jaw, tight upper body, furrowed brow

🌼 *SAD/UNMOTIVATED:* rounded spine, lowered chin, heavy shoulders and head

🌼 *INSECURE/PEOPLE PLEASING:* muscle tension, drooping shoulders, lowered head, constricted throat

🌼 *CALM:* open chest, soft gaze, relaxed muscles

Long-term stress or trauma can lock your body in these patterns, which can affect your mood, which in turn can cause more dysregulation and somatic symptoms and so on . . . a vicious cycle.

Let's change your posture to restore your calm.

1. When you are feeling distressed, press pause and observe your body and posture. Notice your breathing and any tension you are carrying. Notice the position of your spine and shoulders.

2. Shift your posture to a more neutral and safe position, releasing muscle tension as you lengthen your spine (imagine a golden thread gently pulling you up from the crown of your head). Open through your shoulders and heart space, shift your gaze up and drop your shoulders. Relax your jaw.

3. Stay here for 1–5 minutes, breathing nourishing deep breaths and observing any shifts you feel in your mood.

9

BODY SCAN

Body scans build awareness and
connection with your body.

Here's how:

1. Sit somewhere comfortable or lie down.

2. Take a few deep breaths and notice the feeling of your body in contact with the surface beneath it.

3. Start at your feet and begin to move up, mentally scanning each part of your body. Move your attention slowly, pausing to greet and embrace each part of you.

4. If you meet any tension or discomfort you can 'breathe into' this space. Say 'Relax' in your mind as you exhale. Invite your body to surrender, feeling heavy and at ease, or simply observe the tension greeting it with a compassionate 'You are welcome here'.

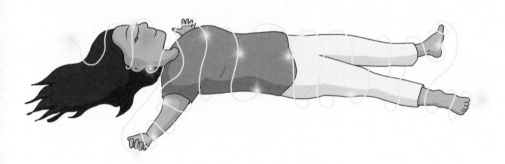

10

EAR MASSAGE

You can create a beautiful sense of calm by massaging your ear. This is a great way to activate your vagus nerve and switch on your parasympathetic nervous system.

This simple technique can be practised discreetly. You may notice signs of release, like a deep spontaneous swallow, a yawn, a sigh, tummy gurgles or a general sense of settling.

Try the following sequence for 30-60 seconds, one ear at a time or both at once.

🌼 *MASSAGE 1*: Press your finger into the little pressure point just under the ridge in your ear and make gentle circles.

🌼 *MASSAGE 2*: Press your finger gently into the pressure point near the ear canal, and make little circles.

🌼 *MASSAGE 3*: Place your pointer and middle finger on the skin behind your ear. You can keep them here or gently massage in an upward motion.

🌼 *MASSAGE 4*: Lightly hold your ear lobe and pull your ear down and away from your skull. Then lightly hold the middle of your ear, pulling out and away. Then the top of your ear, pulling up and away from your head.

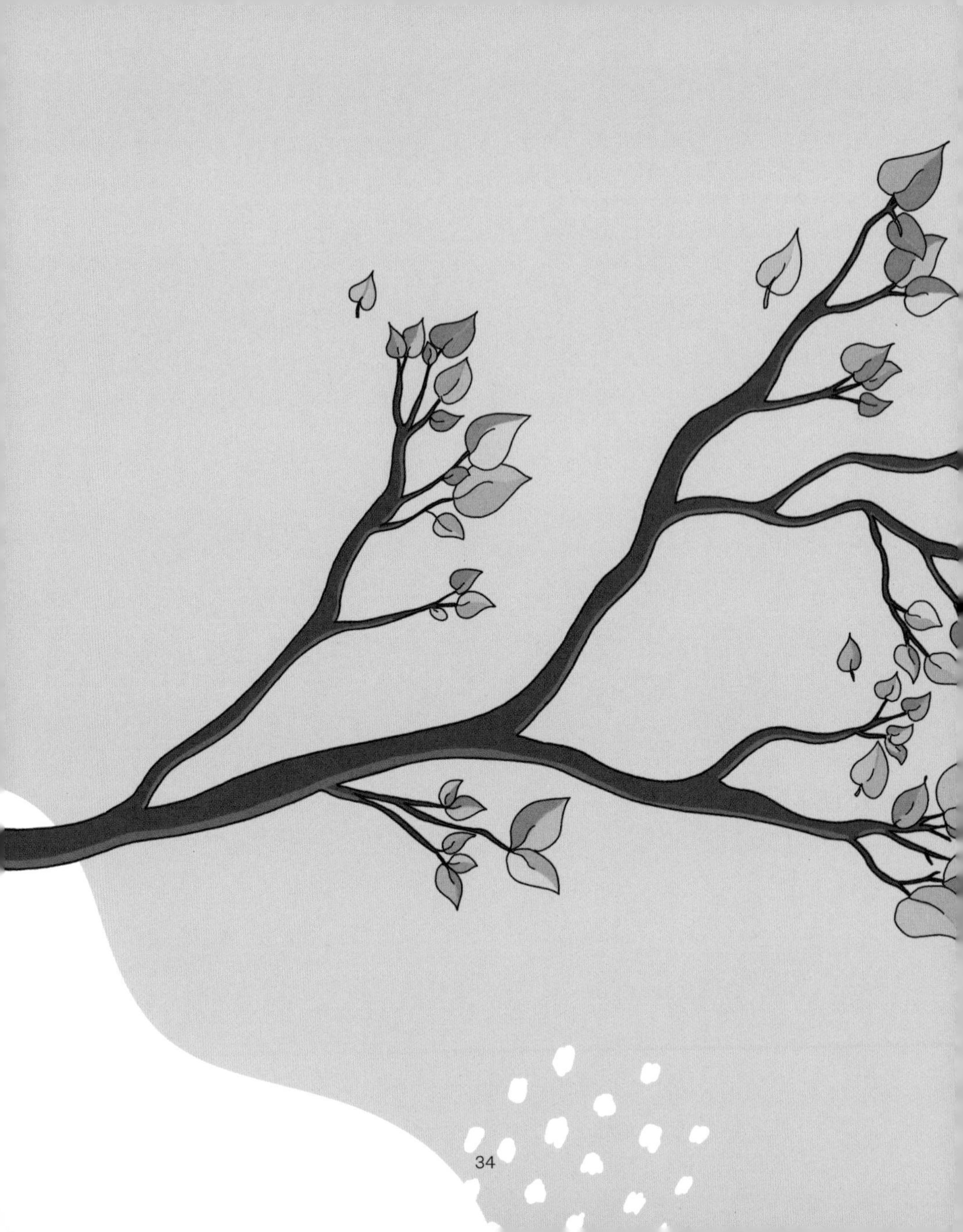

You
deserve a
beautiful
life.

PERIPHERAL VISION

When you feel anxious or panicked you may find your vision changes. It might be hard to make eye contact or your eyes might dart around in search of threats.

Try these practices to send cues
of safety by engaging your vision:

🌸 Slowly scan around your space, taking in your environment. It might help to say a mantra like 'I am here now, safe in this moment', or to look for things in your favourite colour, or to search for items in the room that bring you a sense of joy or calm.

🌸 Keep your head and eyes locked straight ahead while you widen your awareness to notice things at the edge of your vision (in your periphery).

🌸 Hold an object and pass it back and forward slowly between your hands. Move each hand out to the edge of your vision before bringing it back through centre to pass to the other hand. Follow the object with your eyes, while your head remains facing straight ahead.

FACE MASSAGE

The muscles in your face can hold a lot of tension, especially around your forehead and eyes and in your jaw. Soften your expression and find time for some self-love with this practice.

Put some face oil or moisturiser on your fingers so they glide nicely along your skin.

1. Run the pointer and middle finger of both hands up either side of the bridge of your nose, across the tops of your eyebrows and finish with some gentle circles on your temples.

2. Gently 'pinch' and roll the skin of your eyebrows with your thumb on the underside and your pointer finger on top of your eyebrow. Start closest to your nose and work your way to the outer edge of your eyebrows.

3. Massage circles between your eyebrows.

4. Using four fingers of both hands, start in the middle of your forehead and gently sweep outwards and into your hairline.

5. Massage your jaw, starting at the chin and running your fingers along to the edge of your face.

6. Gently massage circles on the jaw joint (near your ears).

7. Lastly, lightly stroke your fingers down both sides of your neck.

13

ARM SQUEEZES

Sometimes when life gets overwhelming you can feel disconnected from your body. The gentle pressure in this lovely technique will help you feel grounded in and connected to your body again.

Here's how:

1. Use your right hand to gently squeeze down the length of each finger on your left hand, then massage your palm.

2. Work your way up your left arm, squeezing the wrist, lower arm, upper arm and into the shoulder and upper trapezius muscle.

3. Repeat on the other side. You can also try this squeezing your legs.

Focus on really feeling the sensations, and continue to breathe with deep inhales and long slow exhales.

14

SOMATIC SHAKING

When we experience a shock, upset or trauma, one of the body's natural responses is to shake. This helps to release stress energy, which 'completes' the stress response and regulates the nervous system.

Intentional shaking can dissolve distress and move your nervous system back to balance if you're feeling hyperaroused (stressed or agitated) so this is a good one to use if you're feeling anxious or triggered.

Here's how:

1. Begin to shake your legs and arms. You can shake one leg at a time, or you can keep both feet on the ground while doing a running motion with the knees.

2. Feel the shaking through your entire body. Play with the intensity and speed so that it feels like a release, rather than further activating.

3. Continue to shake for a minute or so.

4. Come back to stillness. Bring one hand to your belly and the other to your chest, and witness your emotions, your body sensations and your thoughts. Be curious about any changes you feel and breathe deeply to come back to calm.

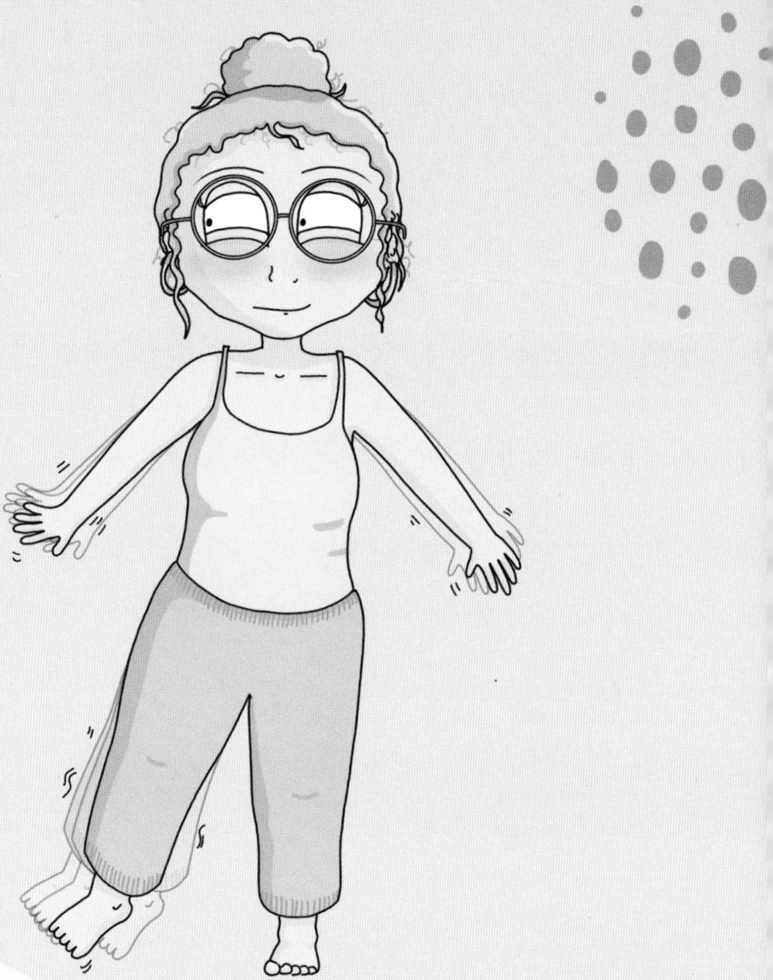

WEIGHTED
BELLY BREATH

This technique calms you by slowing your
breath and providing proprioceptive input.

Here's how:

1. Find an object to place on your belly, like a wheat bag, a hot-water bottle, a heavy blanket or a book.

2. Lie on the ground on your back and place your object on your belly.

3. Begin to deepen your breath, directing your inhale down into your diaphragm. Imagine you have a balloon in your belly that inflates as you inhale, raising your object, and deflates as you exhale, lowering your object. (This is a great way to train your diaphragm muscle for full, functional breathing.)

4. Continue belly-breathing for 3–5 minutes. Notice any changes to your body as your object rises and falls with your breath.

AWARENESS OF BREATH

This is a breath-awareness practice, where you simply notice and meet your breath as it is.

Here's how:

1. Place one hand on your chest and one on your belly.

2. Breathe naturally and begin to observe the sensation under your hands. Which hand seems to be moving more?

3. Notice the air moving in and out of your nostrils. Is it slightly cooler on the inhale, and slightly warmer on the exhale?

When your mind wanders, gently bring your awareness back to your breath.

You don't need to change anything; simply be with your breath, for as long as you like.

17

CHILD'S POSE

This restorative pose allows your mind and body to rest.

Here are three variations to try:

1. Come to kneeling with your big toes touching, your knees out wide, your arms extended forward and your forehead resting on the floor.

2. As for variation 1, but with your knees together.

3. As for variation 2, but with your arms draped alongside your body, palms facing up.

Melt into this nourishing pose for 2–5 minutes, allowing your mind to rest and your thoughts to unravel.

Try out these supports to make child's pose work for you:

❀ Slide a pillow between your calves and glutes or under your belly and chest.

❀ Pop a pillow or block under your forehead if the floor feels too far away.

18

CAT COW

This beautiful movement deepens your
connection to your body, syncing with
your breath for emotional balance.

Here's how:

1. Come to an all fours/table-top position, with your hands and knees on the floor.

2. Inhale as you arch your spine, allowing your belly to dip towards the floor and your chest to open and your head to gaze towards the ceiling.

3. Exhale as you scoop your belly button towards your spine and curve through your spine, tucking your chin towards your chest.

4. Continue, syncing your movements with your slow and steady breath.

You can also try this practice from a seated position with your hands on your knees. Gaze at the ceiling and arch your back as you inhale; round through your shoulders, chin to chest, belly to spine as you exhale.

19

LEGS UP THE WALL

All you need for this practice is a wall!

This practice can help to: calm your mind and nervous system; support your lymphatic system and circulation; slow your breathing; improve digestion; ease back aches; and improve your sleep.

Here's how:

 Lie on your back and scootch your legs up a wall. You can slide a pillow or folded blanket under your hips or drape a blanket over yourself if you like. Settle here for 2–20 minutes.

This tool pairs well with tools #24, #67 and #87.

20

BRiDGE BREATHiNG

A calming movement practice to
synchronise body and breath.

Here's how:

❁ Lie on your back with your feet flat on the floor, knees
pointing to the ceiling, arms alongside your body.

❁ As you inhale, press into your feet to raise your hips off
the ground into a bridge pose. At the same time, raise
your arms to point your hands to the ceiling or all the
way over your head (whatever feels comfortable).

❁ As you exhale, slowly roll your spine down one vertebra
at a time and bring your arms back with you, returning
to your starting position.

❁ Repeat, syncing your movements with your breath.

❁ After a minute or so (or when you've had enough) come
to stillness on your back and feel the calming echoes of
your practice.

ALL EMOTIONS
COME AND GO
LiKE WEATHER
AND THE CLOUDS:

LET THEM BE,
WATCH THEM PASS.
ALL FEELINGS
ARE ALLOWED.

BUTTERFLY

Calm and release tricky emotions while unlocking your hips, where so many emotions can become stuck.

Sit on the floor and bring the soles of your feet together. Allow your knees to fall out to the sides. You can slide pillows under your knees for support if you like.

Stay in this position, or try one of these variations:

🌼 Fold forward so you are draped over towards your feet. Prop yourself up with pillows, bolsters or blocks so that you can sink into the pose without effort. This variation is great if you want to turn inwards and quieten your mind.

🌼 Place a pillow or bolster behind you and lie back onto it. This variation is lovely if you want more expansion and opening through your heart space. It can feel a little vulnerable, so it might feel nice to drape a blanket over yourself.

22

TWISTS

Twists help to bring balance to your nervous system. They are calming when you feel anxious and stressed and uplifting when you feel flat and stuck.

Here are a few ways you can use twists:

❀ **SEATED TWIST:** Come to a seat, inhale deeply and on an exhale bring your left hand to your right knee as you reach your right arm behind you to rest on the floor. Remain fairly upright through your spine. Take two breaths here before exhaling your way back to centre and repeating on the other side. For a more fluid movement, inhale at centre, exhale into the twist, inhale in the twist then exhale back to centre before flowing to the other side.

❀ **STANDING TWIST:** Stand with your feet hip-width apart and begin to rotate from the hips and torso, twisting left and right in a rhythmical sway. Allow your arms to be heavy and to naturally follow your movement, gently tapping the sides of your body.

❀ **SUPINE TWIST:** Lie down and bring the soles of your feet to the floor with your knees pointing to the ceiling. Extend your arms out to the sides. Allow both knees to fall over to your right while keeping your shoulders on the floor (you might need to support your knees with a pillow under them). You can move your head to gaze to the left. Repeat on the other side.

Spend 1–5 minutes practising, imagining that the twist is wringing out anything you no longer want to hold on to, just like wringing water out of a sponge.

23

OCEAN BREATH

Ocean breath (also called Ujjayi breathing)
is a pranayama technique to help you
to feel more calm and centred.

Here's how:

1. Create a gentle constriction in your throat so that your inhale and exhale (through the nose) makes an audible sound like an ocean wave.

2. Notice how your inhale feels cooler in your nostrils, and your exhale feels warmer.

3. You might like to close your eyes and imagine an ocean wave being gently drawn away from the shore on your inhale and then rolling back in to shore over the sand or pebbles as you exhale.

4. Practise for 2–5 minutes.

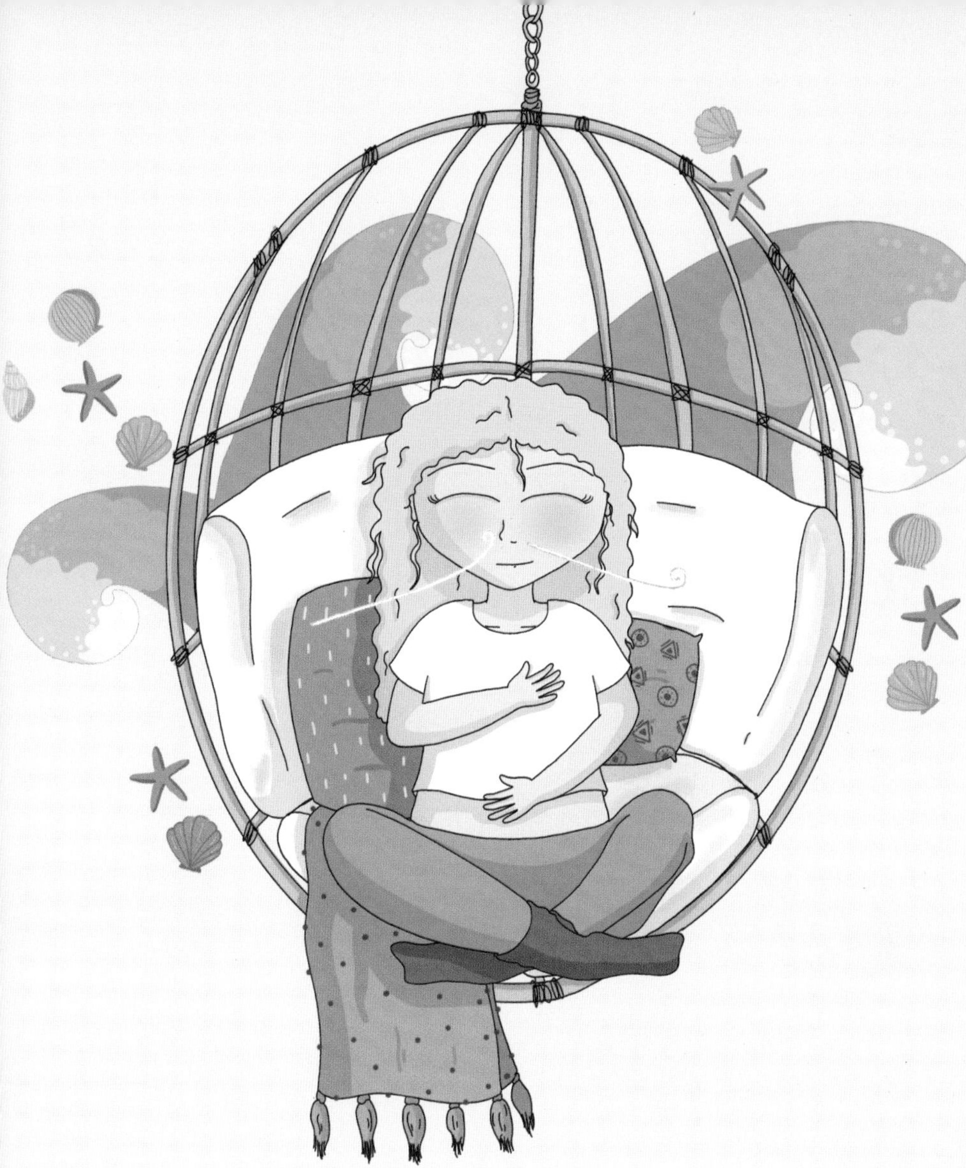

MiNDFUL MUSiC

Most of the time when we listen to music we hear the song as a whole. This tool helps you to use your sense of hearing to experience music in a mindful way.

Pop on a song you love.
As you listen to the music:

🌸 notice the different instruments. Can you pick one and tune in to it for part of the song, then switch to focusing on another instrument?

🌸 if there are lyrics, pay attention to the words.

🌸 take note of the music's speed/tempo.

🌸 notice what emotions come up for you as you listen.

Try this out with different songs and types of music. Notice how the experience changes each time.

MOVING BREATH

Bring some calming and uplifting energy into your day as you sync your breath and body with this moving-breath practice.

Here's how:

1. Come to kneeling.

2. As you inhale, raise up onto your knees and bring your arms out into a cactus position.

3. Slowly exhale, sweeping your arms around alongside your body coming into a child's pose (see tool #17).

Repeat for 1–3 minutes or until you're feeling calm and connected to your body and the present moment.

BREATHiNG-RATE RECORD

This simple exercise provides you with feedback on your breathing rate which can let you know if your body is in a stress response.

Let's find out how many breaths you take per minute.

1. Set a timer on your phone for 1 minute.

2. Start the timer and begin counting your breaths. One breath equals a breath in and a breath out. Breathe normally.

3. When the minute is up, record the number of breaths you took. This is your breaths per minute rate.

A 'normal' breathing rate for an adult who isn't under stress is between 12–16 breaths per minute. If you are nearing 20 breaths or more per minute, you may be over-breathing.

Over-breathing can make you feel faint or lightheaded, and anxious or panicky because the levels of CO_2 and O_2 in your body are out of balance. You end up with less CO_2 than you need; it's the CO_2 that helps your blood vessels dilate so oxygen can be delivered around your body. You might also experience: dizziness or tingling; a tight chest or pain in the chest; frequent yawning or sighing; nausea; bloating; dry mouth; feeling short of breath or that you can't get enough air; a faster heartbeat; or insomnia.

Now, choose a breathing tool (any of these: #15, #38, #75, #76 or #97) and practise for 3–5 minutes.

Next, take your breathing rate again. Chances are it's reduced a good deal.

Slow, controlled (especially diaphragmatic) breathing helps you feel calm and regulated by directly activating your parasympathetic nervous system. If you over-breathe, try this tool three times per day for a week or so, recording your rates and noticing any changes.

27

SAFE PLACE

Create a 'safe place' in your mind. You can return
to this safe space any time you need to 'resource
yourself' and find a sense of peace and calm.

Here's how:

1. Close your eyes and take a few deep breaths.

2. Bring to mind a place that makes you feel content and
   secure. Maybe it's somewhere you've been before or
   maybe it's your very own imaginary haven. You might
   be at the beach, in a cosy armchair by the fire, beside a
   lake, a forest, in a library . . . It doesn't matter where it is,
   as long as it feels safe and calming.

3. Imagine as many details as possible. What do you see,
   hear and smell? What can you touch?

4. Stay here as long as you like and when you are finished,
   slowly open your eyes and return to the room. You can
   return to your safe place at any time.

28

SAVOUR A SCENT

Find something that has a calming scent, like a
candle, a hot chocolate, coffee beans, a flower,
essential oils or moisturiser, and savour it.

Here's how:

1. Close your eyes, bring the object to your nose and
    inhale slowly.

2. Describe the scent to yourself.

3. Notice all the different fragrance notes.

4. What emotion does this scent bring up for you?

5. Do any thoughts or memories arise?

Sit with this exercise as long as you like. You could
also switch to another scented object.

Notice how you feel after a minute or so of
savouring a scent you love.

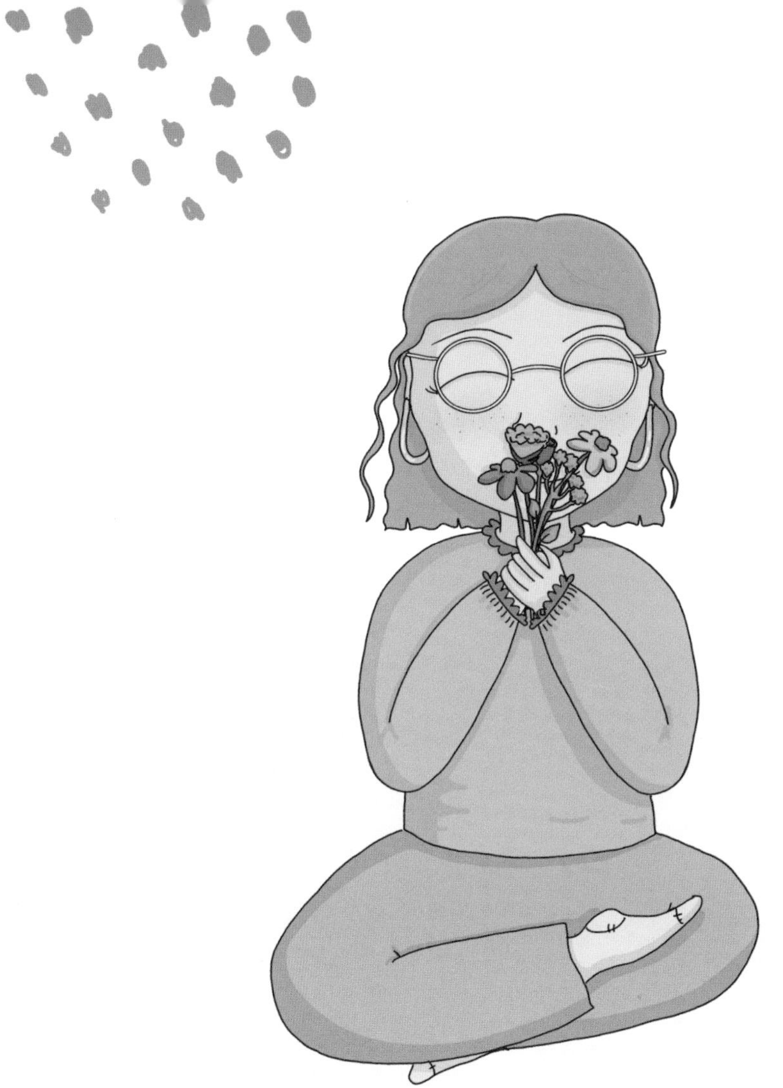

BILATERAL STIMULATION
butterfly taps

Bilateral stimulation helps you to process emotions and memories by activating both hemispheres of your brain. It also helps to centre your focus, providing a gentle way to stay grounded and connected to your body.

Here's how:

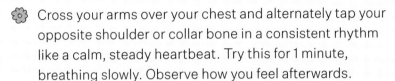 Cross your arms over your chest and alternately tap your opposite shoulder or collar bone in a consistent rhythm like a calm, steady heartbeat. Try this for 1 minute, breathing slowly. Observe how you feel afterwards.

You can call on this tool any time you feel dysregulated. You can also practise this tool while thinking about your safe place (tool #27).

30

BiLATERAL STiMULATiON
thigh taps

Thigh taps are a useful tool for when you're in public and feeling anxious, triggered, overwhelmed or dissociated. No one will know what you're doing! It's especially easy to hide if you're sitting at a desk or table.

Here's how:

❀ Simply place your hands on your thighs and begin to tap back and forth. Keep your rhythm slow and rhythmical like a steady heartbeat.

❀ Make sure you also slow down your breathing, focusing on inhales that expand your diaphragm and side ribs and exhales that are slow and complete.

EMOTIONS AREN'T GOOD
OR BAD, THEY JUST ARE.

WHEN YOU CAN DISENTANGLE
YOURSELF FROM RESISTANCE
AND JUDGEMENT YOU CAN
FIND PEACE AND ACCEPTANCE.

31

BILATERAL STIMULATION finger taps

Here's another great tool for calming anxiety when you're in public!

Here's how:

1. Bring your arms behind your back, crossing them over at the wrists.

2. Begin to alternately tap your thumb against your pointer and middle finger, tapping back and forth between your left and right hands.

3. Make this tapping nice and slow as you calm your breath.

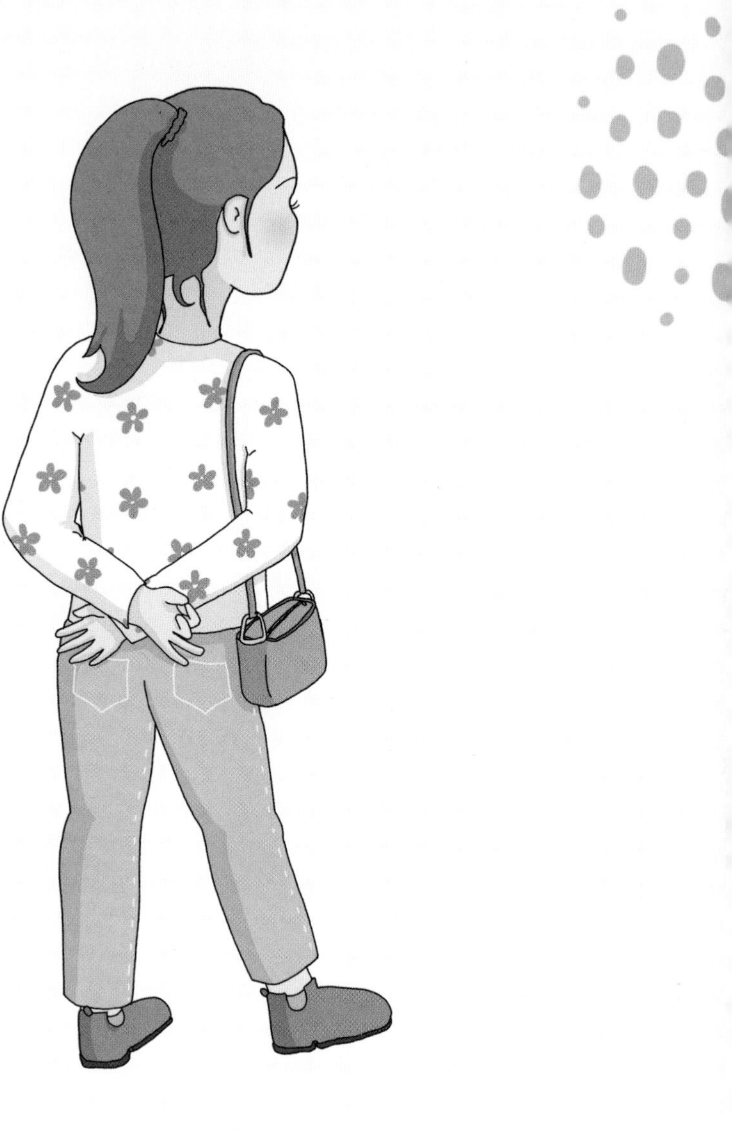

CONTAINMENT HUG

A containment hug (also called a safety hug) has so many benefits: it provides calming proprioceptive input; it anchors you in the here and now; it builds a compassionate connection with your body; and it feels like a loving hug.

Here's how:

🌸 Put your left hand under your right armpit and cross your right arm over the top to hold your left upper arm or shoulder. You might like to close your eyes or lower your gaze and soften your focus.

🌸 Simply breathe in this safe hold as you witness your emotions or thoughts.

🌸 Notice how it feels both to be comforted and to offer yourself comfort.

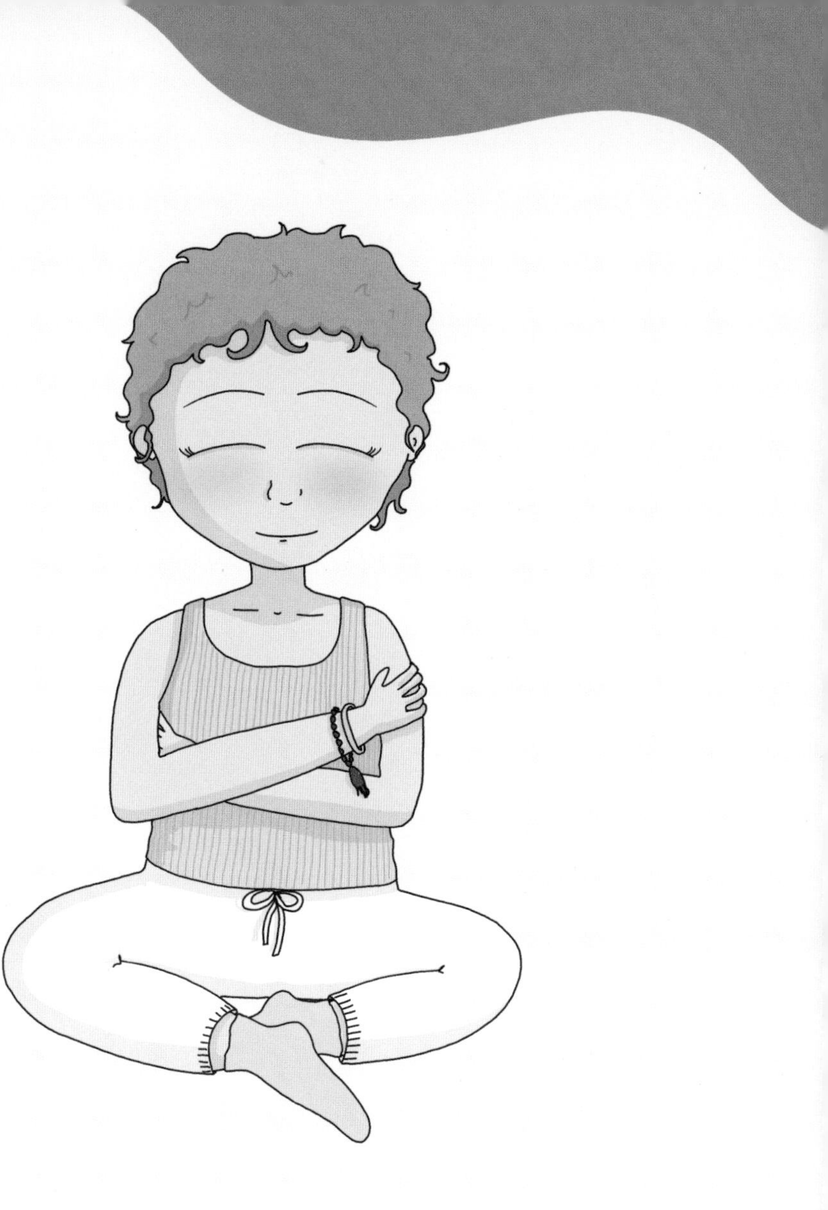

SOMATIC HOLDS

These holds anchor you into your body
and compassionately connect you with
yourself through safe, calming touch.

Here's how:

1. Place your left hand on your heart and your right hand on your belly. Close your eyes if that feels okay, breathe slowly and observe the sensations of your hands against your body. Pay attention to the energetic space between your hands, feeling the connection between your heart and your gut/intuition.

2. Leaving your left hand on your heart, move your right hand to your forehead. Breathe here and feel the connection between your head and heart.

3. Leaving your right hand on your forehead, place your left hand at the base of your skull at the back of your neck. Allow your head to rest back into the support of your left hand. Imagine your mind unwinding and settling here as you breathe slowly into your belly.

VAGUS NERVE EXERCISE

This tool helps to activate your vagus nerve, bringing you back to a calm ventral vagal state. You might notice signs of release like a deep sigh or swallow, a yawn, a general feeling of calm or your tummy gurgling.

Here's how:

1. Tip your head over to the left, bringing your left ear towards your left shoulder (without raising your shoulder).

2. Take your gaze up and to the right.

3. Hold for 30–60 seconds or until you feel a release, then bring your head back to centre.

4. Now tip your head over to the right, bringing your right ear towards your right shoulder.

5. Take your gaze up and to the left.

6. Hold for 30–60 seconds or until you feel a release, then come back to centre.

This makes a great daily practice as a fast and simple way to activate your parasympathetic nervous system.

35

LETTING GO

We hold on to all kinds of things in life: people, old habits, emotions, resentment, limiting beliefs, relationships . . . You really want to just 'get over it' or 'let it go' but it's harder than you thought.

This practice helps to demonstrate some of the nuances around 'letting go'.

Here's how:

1. Grab an object that you can hold in your hand, like a pen.

2. Wrap your hand around the object, holding on tight.

3. Repeat these instructions: 'Do not let this go'; 'Hold on tightly'; 'Do not allow my grip to loosen'.

4. Continue to repeat the instructions, gripping your object for 1 minute.

5. Now let it go. Drop it. Right now.

Do you still feel an imprint of the object on your hand and fingers? Do you notice the 'echoes' of holding onto the object; the sensations of gripping in your hand?

   Did you drop it right away? Or did you pause? Was there a part of you that wanted to hold on, or felt like letting go quickly was tricky?

There is no right or wrong outcome here.

Maybe holding on felt uncomfortable, or even painful? Sometimes you hold onto things even though it doesn't feel good any more.

Letting go isn't always easy either. Often the thing you are trying to let go of is something you have held on to for a long time. Maybe a part of you doesn't want to let go, or is stuck in a pattern of holding on.

When you do let go, you might still feel the imprint of the thing you held on to for quite some time.

When thinking about letting something go, ask yourself:

- Does this still serve me?
- What effect is holding on having on me?
- What is getting in the way of me letting go?
- What might things be like if I let this go?

Remember that what you resist persists. Allow your emotions, and give yourself grace and compassion in your journey of letting go.

36

A-Z DISTRACTION

If you can't go to sleep because your mind
is racing or you need some distraction,
try this brain-refocusing game.

Pick a topic and think of something that begins with
each letter of the alphabet for that topic. You could
choose breeds of dog, fruit and veggies, city names,
insects, restaurant names and so on . . .
    If you lose focus on the game, gently guide your
mind back to it and carry on.

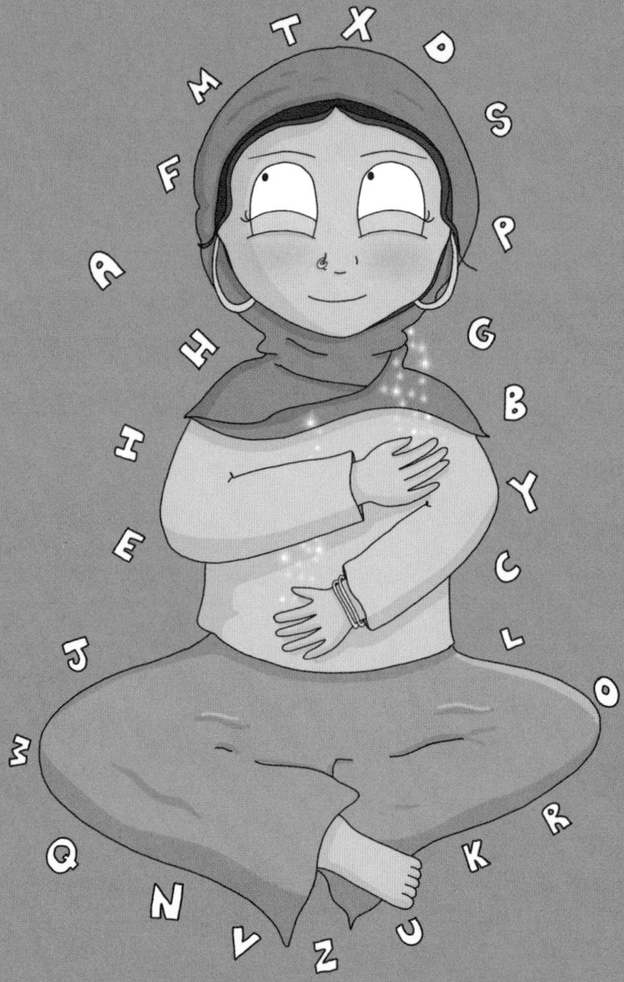
T X D S P G B Y C L O R K U Z V N Q W J E H H A F M

37

THE RIVER OF MIND

Imagine your mind is a river and you
are sitting on the riverbank.

Notice your thoughts flowing by. Sometimes they are busy and fast, rushing by like rapids. Sometimes they are slow and steady, calm like the gentle flow of a stream. Other times your thoughts are like a whirlpool, threatening to suck you in.

Fighting with the flow of the river is what keeps you caught in painful emotional spirals. You can choose not to fight. You are the observer of the river of mind, sitting on the riverbank, taking comfort in simply witnessing the water.

ALTERNATE NOSTRIL BREATHING

This equalising and balancing pranayama breathing technique, also known as Nadi Shodhana, purifies and cleanses the body's energy channels.

Here's how:

1. Sit comfortably with a straight spine.

2. Rest your pointer and middle fingers between your eyebrows. You will use your thumb and ring fingers to alternately close and release your nostrils.

3. Exhale fully then use your right thumb to close your right nostril.

4. Inhale through your left nostril then close your left nostril with your ring finger.

5. Release your right nostril and exhale.

6. Inhale through your right nostril then close your right nostril with your thumb.

7. Release your left nostril and exhale.

8. Go back to step 4 and repeat.

Spend 3–5 minutes with this beautiful breath practice which calms and settles your mind, body and emotions by balancing both hemispheres of the brain.

FIVE-FINGER BREATH

Start with your pointer finger resting in the middle of the crease of your other hand's palm and wrist. Inhale as you slowly trace out to your thumb and exhale as you slowly trace back to your starting point.

Continue slowly inhaling and exhaling until you have traced up and down each finger.

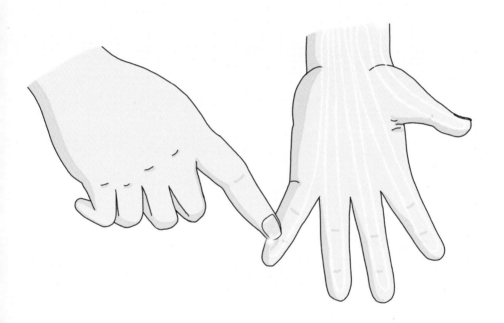

SOMATIC SENSATIONS

In order to process emotions and regulate your nervous system you need to be connected to your body. This means: noticing the sensations you are experiencing; describing and sitting with them as their witness; and breathing into them and allowing them to pass through. This list will help you name and describe the body sensations you feel. It's a great resource to use in tools like #9, #41, #60, #71 and #93.

Tune in to your body and ask yourself 'What has my attention in this moment?' Describe those sensations to yourself.

Achy	Buzzing	Cozy	Elastic
Airy	Chilled	Cramped	Electric
Alive	Clammy	Cut off	Empty
Bloated	Closed	Dense	Energised
Blocked	Cold	Disappearing	Expanding
Breathless	Congested	Dissolving	Explosive
Brittle	Constricted	Dizzy	Faint
Bubbly	Contracted	Drained	Flowing
Burning	Cool	Dull	Fluid

Flushed	Knotted	Radiating	Stuck
Fluttery	Light	Ragged	Suffocating
Frantic	Limp	Raw	Sweaty
Frozen	Loose	Releasing	Swirling
Full	Nauseous	Rolling	Tender
Fuzzy	Nervy	Shaky	Tense
Goose Bumpy	Numb	Sharp	Thick
Gurgling	Open	Shimmering	Throbbing
Hard	Paralysed	Shivery	Tickly
Heavy	Pit in stomach	Shudder	Tight
Hollow	Pounding	Silky	Tingling
Hot	Pressure	Smooth	Trembling
Icy	Prickly	Soft	Twitchy
Imploding	Puffy	Spacious	Untethered
Intense	Pulled	Spasming	Vibrating
Itchy	Pulsing	Sticky	Warm
Jagged	Quaking	Still	Weak
Jittery	Queasy	Stretchy	Wobbly
Jumbly	Quiet	Stringy	
Jumpy	Quivering	Strong	

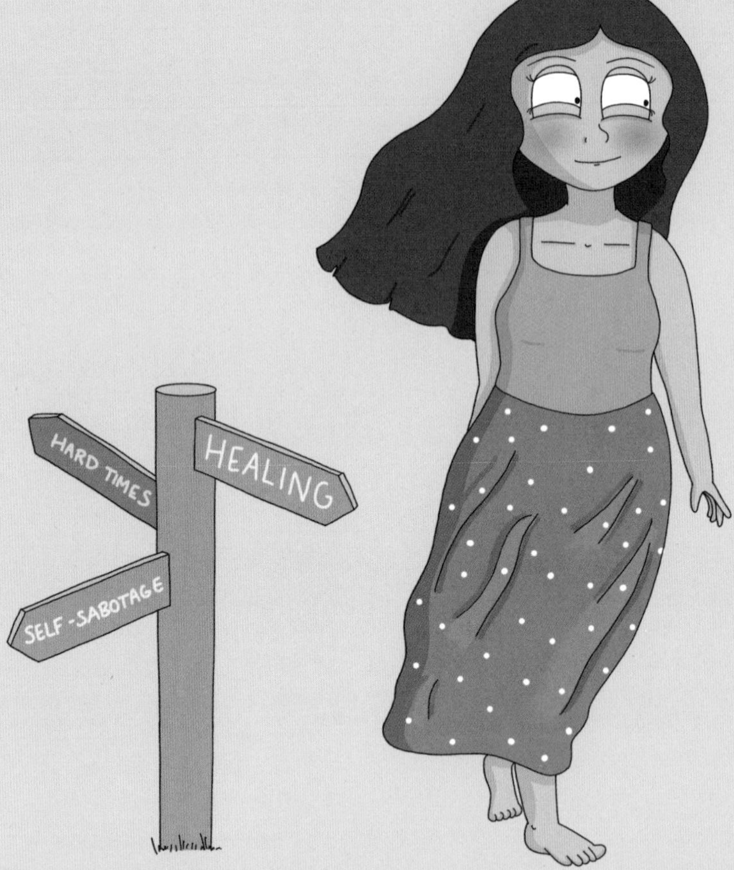
HARD TIMES
HEALING
SELF-SABOTAGE

YOU HAVE
SURViVED EVERY
HARD THiNG YOU
HAVE EVER BEEN
THROUGH.

BOUNDARY SENSING

For this exercise you will need to find three objects: an object that you love (a 'yes' object), an object that you feel neutral about and an object you strongly dislike or that disgusts you (a 'no' object). For example, you might love your blanket, feel neutral about your water bottle and hate the feeling of the dirty dish sponge.

Here's what to do with your objects:

1. Line each object up in front of you. Notice which one you are drawn to touch first. How do you know this?

2. Pick up your 'yes' object. Bring it to your face, smell it, feel it. What does a 'yes' feel like in your body? Notice subtle body cues: facial expressions, movements and emotions.

3. Now do the same with your neutral object.

4. Finally turn to your 'no' object. Notice what your body does. What does a 'no' feel like in your body? Think about picking it up, bringing it to your face, smelling and touching it. How does your body respond to this? Notice the subtle body cues again.

This exercise helps you to tune in to your body, your boundaries and your 'no'. When you learn what this feels like in your body, you can look out for this in your life with people, commitments, demands and where you put your time.

If you have suppressed or numbed your emotions, or been caught in cycles of people pleasing, it isn't uncommon to feel disconnected from your needs. Tuning in to your body in this way will reconnect you with your emotions and intuition.

42

HEALiNG BREATH

Take a cosy seat and get ready to learn this beautiful breath practice to compassionately connect with your body, process emotions and dissolve pain and tension.

Here's how:

1. Close your eyes or lower your gaze and take a scan through your body. Notice if there are any sensations or emotions calling for your attention.

2. If you are noticing an emotion, describe where you feel this in your body. What colour is it? How big is it? What shape is it? What texture is it? If you are noticing a sensation (pain, tension, niggles), describe it. (See tool #40 if you need some help.)

3. Begin to 'breathe into' this emotion or sensation, visualising your inhale filling up or wrapping around it. Picture your exhale cleansing and dissolving any tension or discomfort.

4. Imagine a healing golden light coming down from above to fill and infuse this space, soothing and dissolving any distress or discomfort.

5. Continue to breathe into this area, allowing your inhale to fill and nourish you and your exhale to release anything you no longer need. Each exhale also invites a deeper sense of relaxation and ease, creating lightness and expansion within you.

6. Stay here for as long as you need, or until you feel some release.

FEELING THE BREATH

This is a breath awareness practice, which means you don't need to change your breath in any way. You simply observe your breath as it is, without judgement.

Here's how:

1. Bring your attention to your breath as a whole for a few moments. Notice the quality of your breath. Is it shallow or deep? What sensations do you notice in your throat, chest and belly?

2. Shift your focus to your nostrils. Notice your breath entering and exiting your nostrils. You might notice that your inhale feels slightly cool and your exhale feels warm.

3. Shift your focus to your chest, perhaps bringing one hand to rest over your heart space. Observe the rise and fall of your chest as you breathe.

4. Focus now on the sides of your ribcage. Place one or both hands over the sides of your ribs and notice the movement of your breath against them.

5. Bring your hands to your belly and tune in to any movement of the breath you feel here. Perhaps you might notice your belly rise with your inhale and fall with your exhale. Just be with your breath as it is.

You can shift between these focal points (nostrils, chest, ribs and belly) for as long as you like.

JOG AND FOLD

This practice can help you to complete
the stress response if you've been holding
back anger or feeling anxious.

Here's how:

1. Jog on the spot for 1 minute.

2. Stop. Inhale deeply then exhale into a forward fold.
   Hang like a rag doll, with a slight bend in your knees.
   Sway your upper body side to side. Stay here for
   30–60 seconds.

It might feel good to
follow this up with tool
#53 or a breathing
tool like #15 or #38.

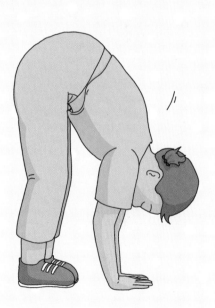

ROCK AND TILT

Create space and emotional release
in your hips with this practice.

Here's how:

Sit on the ground. Bring the soles of your feet together to touch and allow your knees to fall out to the sides in a butterfly pose.

🌼 **VARIATION 1:** Holding your feet or lower legs, begin to rock side to side. Enjoy this gentle, rhythmical sway.

🌼 **VARIATION 2:** Holding your feet or lower legs, inhale as your belly expands and tilt your pelvis forward. Exhale and tilt your pelvis back (rolling onto your tailbone), and gently pull your belly in towards your spine.

Choose the variation you prefer and repeat for 1–5 minutes.

HEEL DROPS

This practice relieves stress and anxiety
by calming your nervous system while
connecting you to the earth and your body.

Here's how:

1. Begin standing, and allow your eyes to defocus.

2. Rise up onto your toes and then let yourself thud back
   down to your heels.

3. Continue at a slow rhythm for 1 minute, noticing the
   sensations in your legs, hips and lower back.

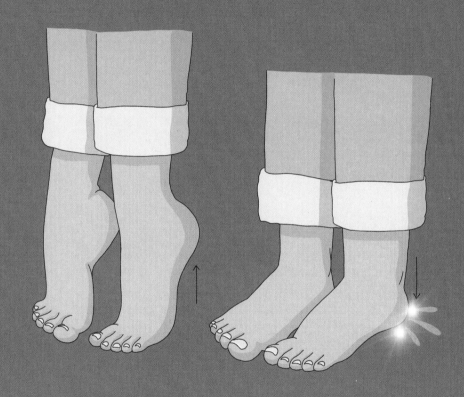

WALL PUSH

Often you need to express anger to complete your body's response to stress. That's okay! So find an unsuspecting wall, and push against it with all your might.

This is a great way to let your muscles use some energy and also to imagine yourself setting a boundary, pushing away anything you don't want in your life.

Afterwards it might feel good to shake out your arms and legs then place one hand on your heart and one hand on your belly to connect with your breath and the message that anger is trying to send you.

Other ways to release anger: pillow punches; throw a pillow down onto the ground repeatedly; scream into a pillow; clench your fists; shake your body (tool #14); throw ice cubes at a brick wall or onto concrete; rip up paper; dance wildly around the room to music or wring out a towel with your hands.

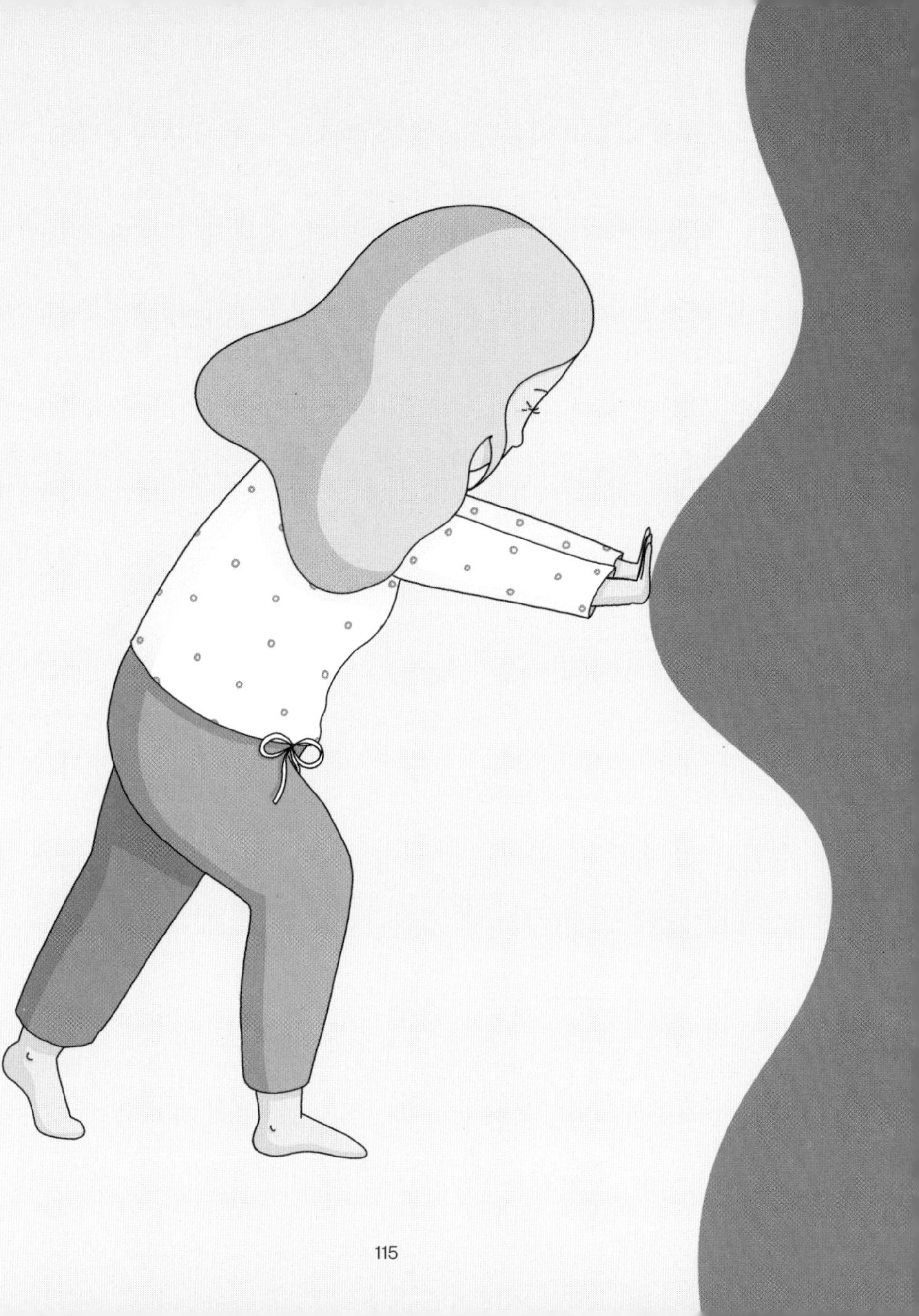

48

ENERGY SHiELD

Create an energy boundary, to create some
space between you and 'not you'. This is ideal
for 'people pleasers' and people who tend to
absorb the energy and emotions of others.

Stand tall and start pushing your hands through the air in different
directions, like you are pushing through water, so you can feel
your power meeting a gentle sense of resistance. Imagine you are
creating an energy shield or that there is a clear Perspex boundary
around your body protecting you.

Next, gently pat and press your hands over your body: down
your arms, legs, chest and so on. Feel the physical boundary lines
of your body, the place where you end and 'not you' begins.

Remind yourself of this protective boundary when you are
around others who tend to leave you feeling drained.

You can say to yourself during this practice: 'This is my body.
These are my emotions. I have the power to choose what I allow in
and what stays separate from me.'

49

VOCAL-CHORD CALMING

Vocalising helps to activate and tone your vagus nerve. Your vagus nerve runs through your neck alongside your larynx and pharynx, so when you sing, hum, chant or gargle, your vocal cords vibrate and wake it up. This tool is also useful to engage your voice to help you shift out of a fawn response (people pleasing) and into expressing your boundaries and needs.

Try:

- ✿ humming along to your favourite song
- ✿ gargling water for 30–60 seconds (you could piggy back this on to an existing habit by doing this each time you shower or brush your teeth)
- ✿ singing
- ✿ chanting 'om' or 'voo' on a long exhale.
- ✿ exhaling while making the sound 'mmmm'
- ✿ exhaling slowly with a loud and extended 'shhhh' sound (this helps to open the diaphragm and release tension and emotions that can be trapped in the body).

50

COLD

Cold water is a powerful tool to
soothe the nervous system.

Here are a few different ways to use cold water:

🌸 Cold water plunge (by far the most daring!): Immerse yourself in cold water such as a cold bath or an ocean dip.

🌸 Cold shower: Turn your shower to cold for a 30-second blast.

🌸 Cold water face dunk: Fill up a bowl or sink with cold water (you can add some ice cubes). Take a breath and submerge your face (up to your cheekbones/temples). Aim for 15–30 seconds (or as long as you can hold it). Repeat a few times. You can also hum slowly in the water to exhale.

🌸 Run an ice cube over your wrist, upper lip or on the back of your neck or hold it in your mouth.

🌸 Hold something frozen against the back of your neck or on your chest for 30 seconds.

🌸 Run your wrists under the cold tap or splash cold water on your face.

Why cold water? When your face comes into contact with cold water it activates the body's natural response to conserve oxygen. This is called the mammalian diving reflex. Your heart rate very quickly lowers by up to 25 per cent, which makes these techniques especially powerful for calming panic attacks and anxiety and lowering stress, while grounding you back in your body in the here and now.

PRACTICE iN
THE CALM TO ACCESS
iN THE CHAOS.

By building a regular practice of tools to regulate your nervous system you create pathways in your brain that become habits.

This way, not only do you rewire your body, brain and baseline, but when you are dysregulated you are able to call on your tools to help you find calm.

51

CANDLE INTENTIONS

Time to explore a delicious candle-lighting
ritual; a safe space to set intentions,
practise mindfulness and just be.

Find a cosy nook to set up one or more candles. Make it as indulgent and lush as you like (think essential oils, soft pillows, snuggly socks, comfortable clothes, calming music and dim lighting).

Before you light the candle, set an intention. Maybe it is to foster more self-compassion? Maybe it is to sit with a tricky emotion? Maybe you want to release something that no longer serves you?

When you have your intention in mind, light your candle to symbolise bringing this intention into focus.

Witness and accept whatever comes up. Mindfully observe thoughts, emotions and body sensations. Watch them as they arrive and notice as they ebb, flow and maybe dissolve thanks to your non-judgemental attention.

You can journal about your intention or just embrace whatever experience you have.

When you have spent the time you need, or found some release, relief or resolution, you could say 'I honour myself and my intention' or 'I release this and return to my day' and then blow out the candle to symbolise the end of your practice.

52

SWAY

**There's a reason people sway when they
hold an upset baby or child; this movement
helps you feel safe and soothed.**

You can be seated or standing as you begin to gently
sway side to side.

Sync this movement with your breath. Close your eyes
if you like.

Make it extra nourishing by humming a gentle
'mmmm' sound or sighing on your exhale.

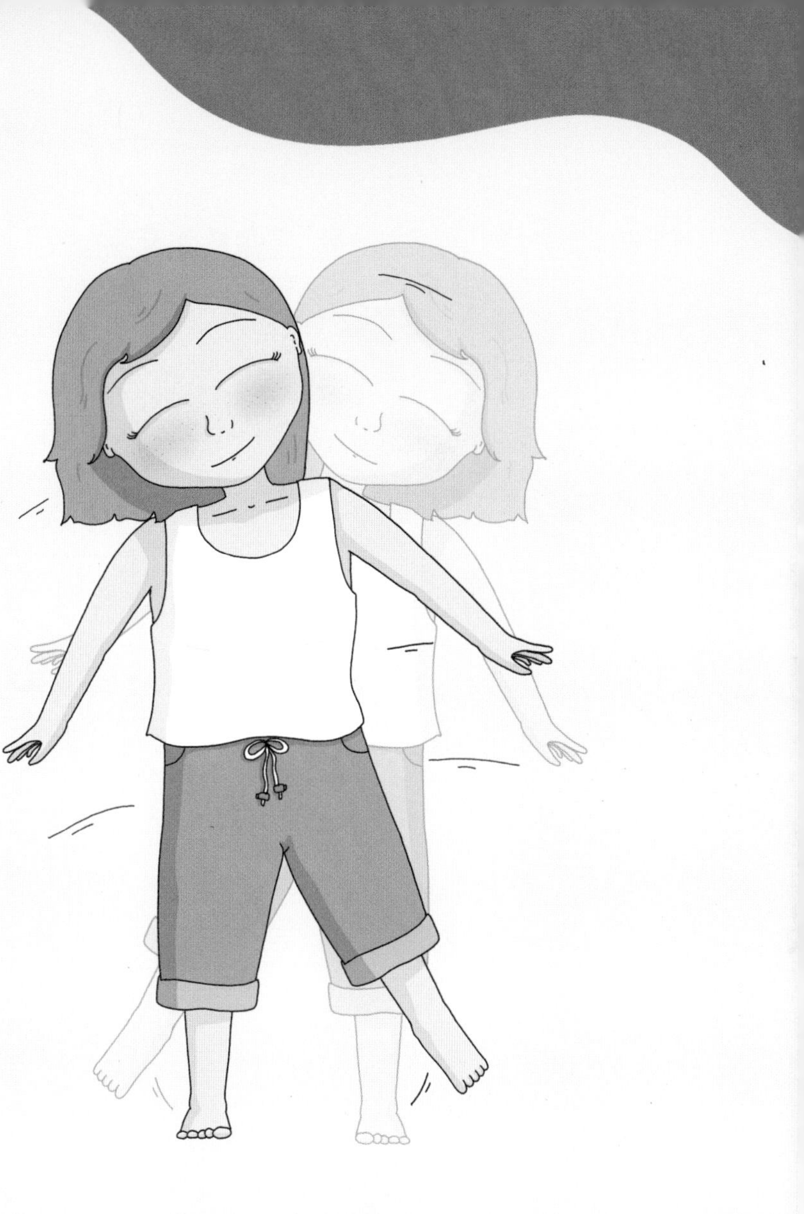

HIP ROCKS

Hip rocks are a great release for both tricky emotions and your lower back.

Here's how:

1. Lie on the ground on your belly.

2. Rest your head down on your hands and breathe deeply, feeling your belly press into the floor on an inhale and soften away on an exhale.

3. Rock your hips side to side in a comfortable rhythm. Find a pace that feels as effortless as possible. Continue to breathe deeply here for about 60 seconds, allowing your full attention to rest on the movement and your body.

4. Come to stillness and observe the echos of this practice in your body and on your emotions.

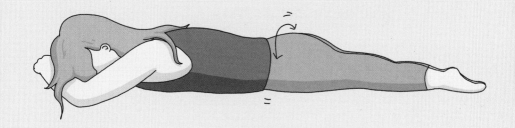

54

LOW STIMULATION
SENSORY SHOWER

Many people rush through their showers, with their minds on other things. This low-stimulation shower invites you to linger with your senses, melting tension away and restoring calm.

Pick and choose from these ideas:

✿ Turn the lights off in the bathroom. Either have a light on outside the room and the door ajar or light some candles.

✿ Pick a temperature that isn't too hot or too cold.

✿ Lower the shower pressure to a gentle rainstorm.

✿ Pop some drops of your favourite essential oil on a washcloth on the shower floor or use a shower steamer infused with soothing scents (see page 132 for some helpful suggestions).

✿ Enjoy the silence or turn on some calming music.

✿ Take your time, slowly and gently washing your body. Listen to the sound of the water, inhale and savour the scents of the steamer or shower products.

✿ As you wash, say a few words of gratitude to each part of your body.

55

AROMA BOMBS

Shake a couple of essential oil drops into the palm of your hands, or mix a couple of drops in a carrier oil like almond oil. Cup your hands together, making a little space between your thumbs for your nose. Take a lovely deep inhale of the aroma bomb.

Try:

- peppermint for when you're feeling down or low on energy.

- lavender, sandalwood, orange, lemon or ylang ylang for anxiety, worry and panic.

- ylang ylang, lemongrass, rose or chamomile for when you're feeling angry.

- clary sage, bergamot, rosemary or lavender for stress.

- bergamot, ginger, lavender or lemon for grief.

- mandarin, sandalwood, jasmine or vetiver for dissociation and grounding.

56

CONNECT

A safe and warm connection with
someone you trust provides co-regulation;
you get to 'borrow' their calm.

When you are stuck in a rut and feeling down or blue you
might notice that you withdraw from others. You may find
that you isolate yourself and have no energy or motivation
for being around people.

When you feel regulated, you feel more open to socialising;
likewise being around people who are supportive and uplifting
will help you to feel more calm, resilient and connected.

Think of someone who feels safe, caring and loving.
You could reach out and connect with them, in person or
by message.

You can also imagine spending time in the loving presence
of someone (even someone who has passed). What would they
say to you? How would you feel if you were with them? Imagine
their warm smile, kind eyes and maybe a hug or their hand on
your shoulder.

You deserve support and love.

57

DRAW YOUR EMOTION

You don't need to be an artist! Grab some paper and get out of your head by intuitively drawing your emotion.

How big is it? What colour is it? What texture is it? What shape is it? Are the lines soft or heavy, flowing or jagged?
    This technique is a useful way of expressing and processing your feelings, even if you're not sure exactly which emotion you're experiencing.

GROUND iN NATURE

Nature soothes and heals.

A quick change of environment can help you manage overwhelming emotions. Pause what you are doing and step outside.

You could take a nature walk or stroll around the block. It might be as simple as standing barefoot on your back lawn for 2 minutes, closing your eyes and breathing fresh air deep into your lungs, as you notice the air against your skin.

Wherever you are, scan for nature's colours and patterns, and tune in to the sounds around you.

59

PHYSIOLOGICAL SIGH

Have you ever noticed the double inhale followed by the long sighing exhale that happens after an emotional release like a big cry? This instinctual recalibrating breath is called a physiological sigh. It is a rapid way to calm anxiety and soothe your nervous system.

Here's how:

1. Inhale through your nose, almost to full capacity, then take a second smaller 'top-up' inhale.

2. Sigh out in one long exhale through your mouth.

3. Drop your shoulders . . . and any unhelpful thoughts you're holding on to while you're at it.

4. Repeat several times or continue for a few minutes.

60

NAME YOUR EMOTION

Naming your emotions is healing and helpful. It allows you to create space for how you feel while you are processing the emotion. Externalising emotions helps to down-regulate the limbic system and amygdala.

How do you name your emotions? How do you even know what you are feeling?

Let's start with the body. Pause for a moment, and take a deep breath. Close your eyes if that feels okay and begin to scan your body. Tune in to whatever is present for you in this moment.

Describe your body sensations, simply noticing without judgement or resistance. (You might like to head back to tool #40 for help.) Spend some time here, witnessing your body sensations and watching as they change. They may come and go, fade or get more intense. It's all okay.

Now ask yourself 'What is my general emotional sense?' Is there an overall positive, neutral or uncomfortable quality to this feeling? Do you have a sense of one or more specific emotions? What clues does your body give you about this?

 Feeling a bubbly warmth in your chest or belly might be happiness, joy or excitement.

❀ Feeling a heavy, dropping or flipping feeling in your tummy might be anxiety or anticipation.

❀ Noticing a heavy, tight feeling in your chest might be stress, anxiety, overwhelm or grief.

❀ Observing heavy or hollow sensations might be sadness.

❀ Feeling a light, expansive feeling in your chest might be calm, and so on.

Have a shot at naming your emotion. You don't need to 'get it right' and in fact, once you say it out loud you might realise that it doesn't quite fit, which is helpful information, too. Perhaps your emotion is quite general, such as 'I'm noticing a positive or neutral feeling'.

If this emotion was in front of you, how would you describe it? How big is it? What colour? What shape? What texture?

If you feel overwhelmed, open your eyes and orient yourself to the space around you or pause the exercise to walk around and have a drink of water.

A good practice for naming emotions is to frame it like this: 'I am noticing . . .' For example 'I am noticing anxiety' rather than 'I am anxious.' This helps to create a little space between you and the emotion. It honours that you are not your emotions; you are the container that is holding space for a passing experience.

Sit with the emotion for as long as you like. When you are ready, you might like to bring yourself back to the present with a grounding exercise such as tool #29, #32 or #58.

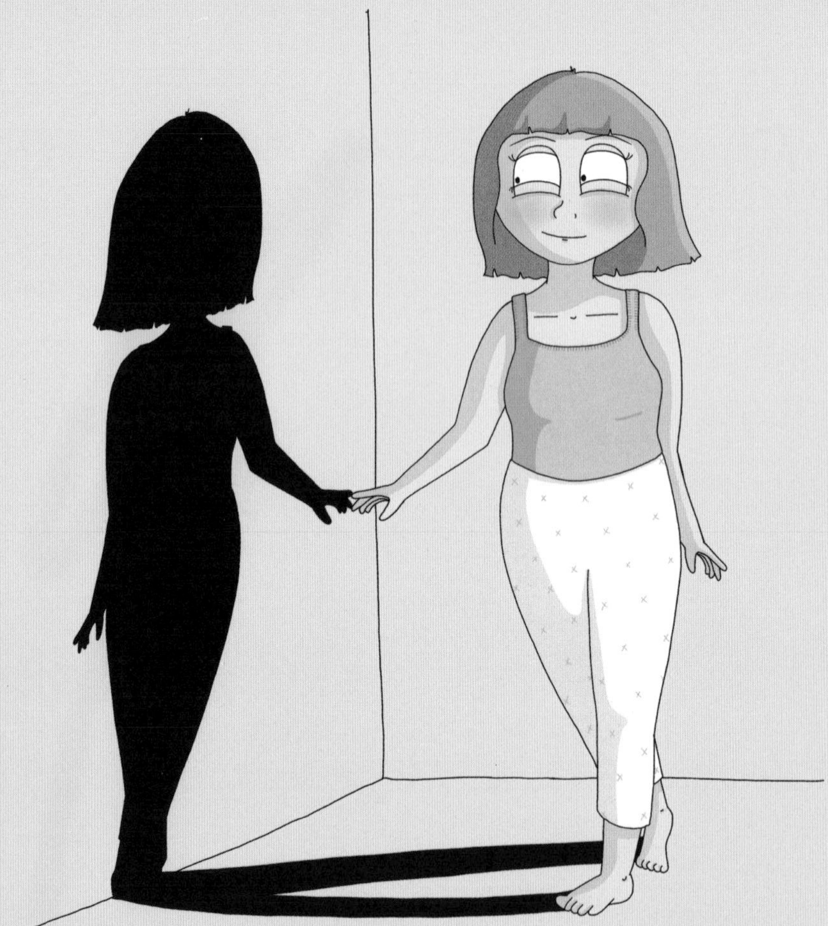

We all have 'shadow parts' — the parts we don't feel proud of and try to hide. Be curious about these parts; they often initially came to be in order to protect you. Show them compassion, understanding and acceptance, rather than banishing them with judgement and shame. This is how you'll find healing and peace.

61

HOT-SPOT SCAN

'Hot spots' are places in the body that hold anxiety, anger and stress. If you hold tension in your body, the body sends a message to your brain that you are in danger, keeping you stuck in a stress-tension feedback loop and creating long-term pain in your body.

A regular hot-spot scan can help you to relax and begin to rewire your nervous system.

Scan the following areas several times a day:

- ❋ *FOREHEAD*: between your eyes
- ❋ *JAW*: notice clenching
- ❋ *SHOULDERS*: notice hunching and tension
- ❋ *CHEST*: notice constriction
- ❋ *BELLY*: notice bracing and 'sucking in'
- ❋ *GLUTES*: notice gripping.

As you scan, 'breathe into' any tension then soften, drop and release.

62

BURRITO WRAP

This tool provides comforting proprioceptive input to calm your senses and soothe the nervous system to restore balance and peace.

Here's how:

1. Grab a cosy blanket.

2. Wrap it around yourself, rolling yourself up like a burrito.

3. Make sure your arms feel tucked in and snug.

4. Sit or lie down and breathe slowly into your belly.

5. Close your eyes and focus on your breath and the 'hugging' sensation of your blanket 'burrito wrap'.

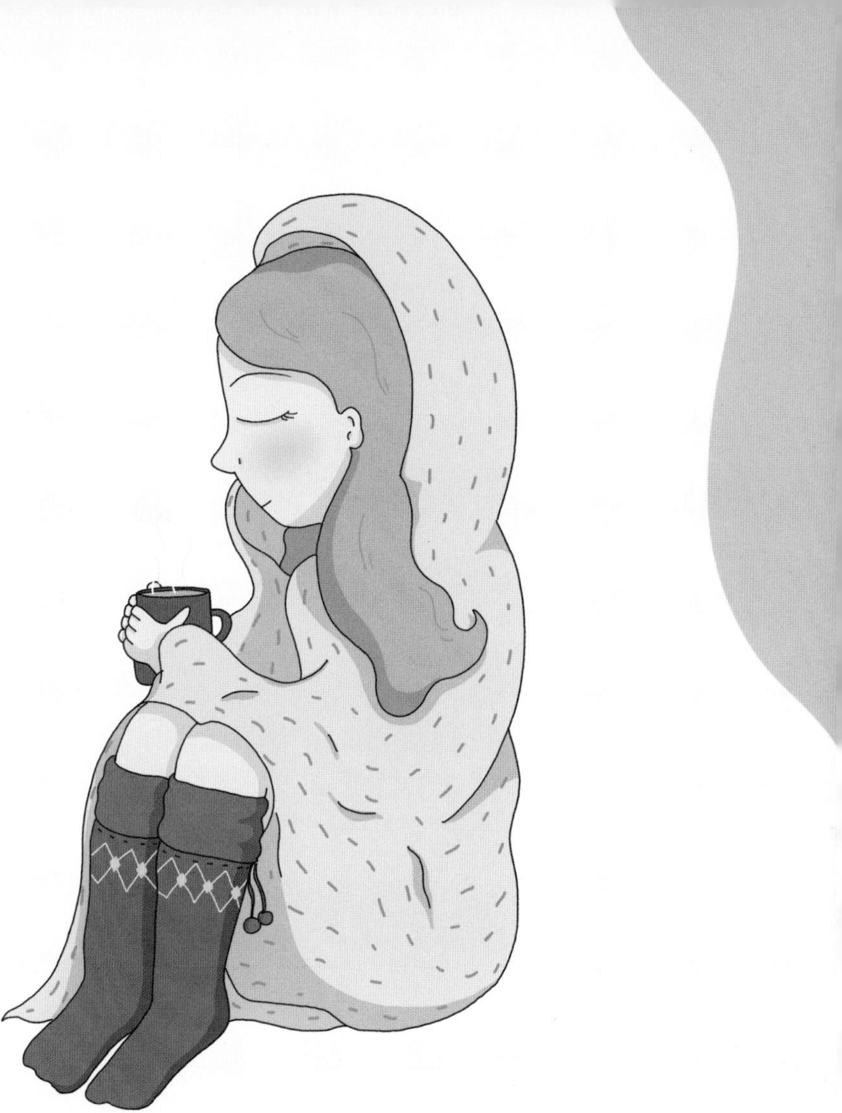

5, 5 OR 5 TOOL

The 5, 5 or 5 tool helps with procrastination and overwhelm and can kick-start your motivation. Which 5 will you choose?

5 seconds

When you think about a positive behaviour, take action within 5 seconds.

Have the idea to go for a walk? Stand up and put your shoes on right away. Think you should tidy up the lounge? Pick up something within 5 seconds and put it away.

If you are feeling unmotivated and think about doing something helpful or productive but then don't act quickly, chances are you'll talk yourself out of it.

Your brain loves comfort and familiarity. It likes to take the habitual, easy path, which is usually staying firmly on the couch or continuing to mindlessly stare at your screen.

Acting quickly breaks that circuit. Even though you may not enjoy it, you will feel a sense of positivity and achievement afterwards.

5 things

When you have a big task at hand or a full to-do list it's easy to get overwhelmed and not take any action at all.

This tool asks you to break your tasks down into manageable chunks and do just five of them. You could complete five paragraphs of your work project, read five pages of your book, pick up and put away five things in your house . . .

The momentum of doing something will often motivate you to keep going.

5 minutes

Give yourself full permission to do just 5 minutes of a task and then stop. Five minutes walking, working, cleaning . . .

Maybe you will be motivated to carry on. But if not, it's okay to stop after 5 minutes. After all, that's five more minutes than you would have done otherwise.

POST-ITS

Post-It Notes are a nifty hack that can have a powerful impact on your ability to create and stick to new habits.

How often do you learn a new tool (like the 101 tools in this book) that you swear you're going to start using, only to realise days later that you've stopped doing it or maybe never even started? If this resonates with you, you're not alone! Brains love familiar, easy tasks, and sometimes put new habits in the too-hard basket.

Post-It Notes could be the jump-start your brain needs. You can write a simple reminder on them or nothing at all. The Post-It alone is the signal to engage in the habit.

This works especially well when the Post-Its are:

- 🌼 linked to a habit that won't take long to complete

- 🌼 stuck in spots where you are most likely to follow through with the habit

- 🌼 moved to a new spot after a week (otherwise your brain gets used to seeing them somewhere and begins to ignore them).

Here are some ideas:

❀ Put a Post-It on your bathroom mirror. Every time you see it, say something you are grateful for.

❀ Slap a Post-It on your car's dashboard to remind you to take five deep belly breaths.

❀ Pop a Post-It in beside your kettle. Every time you boil the kettle for a cuppa, the Post-It reminds you to listen to the water boiling and practise calming (vagus nerve) exercises (see tools #10, #34 and #49).

Do you have a simple habit you would like to incorporate into a daily practice? Grab some Post-Its and pop them around your house today.

65

BRAIN DUMP

A brain dump can clear your racing mind of worries,
stop rumination and help you to switch off.

Here's how:

✿ Get a piece of paper and start a timer for 5–15 minutes.

✿ Jot down each and every thought that pops into your
mind. You can also scribble, draw and use single words.

✿ Note down repeat thoughts and 'my mind is blank'
thoughts. Try to write continuously in a 'stream of
consciousness' style.

✿ When the timer finishes, stop writing.

You might like to review your brain dump, perhaps
making a plan to tackle your worries, burning the paper
to 'let go' of everything it holds, or picking one thing
from the paper to get started on.

JUST ONE THING

When you're feeling overwhelmed or low, wondering how to get back on top of things feels completely daunting.

When your mood is a 2 out of 10, you can get caught in the trap of dwelling on all the steps it will take to get back to a 10. This approach can make you feel helpless and hopeless. Instead, focus on moving just one point up the scale. How might you move from a 2 to a 3?

Ask yourself, 'What is one thing I could do for myself right now that would move me in a helpful direction?' If you focus on one thing at a time, you are much more likely to gain some traction.

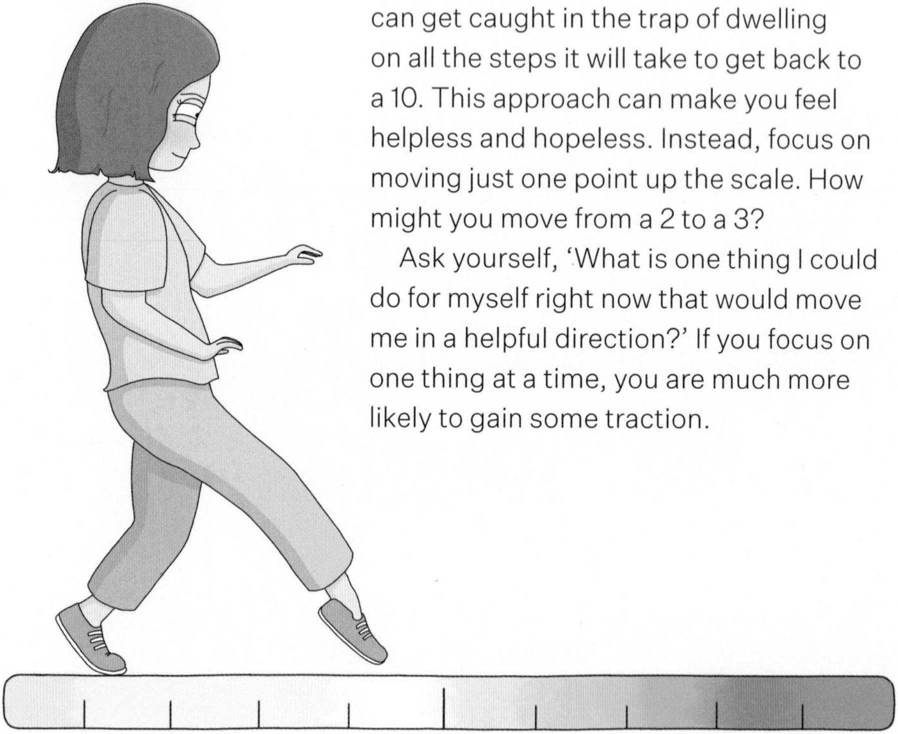

Here's a 'random tool picker' to get you started. Close your eyes, hover your finger above the page, drop it down and try whichever tool you land on.

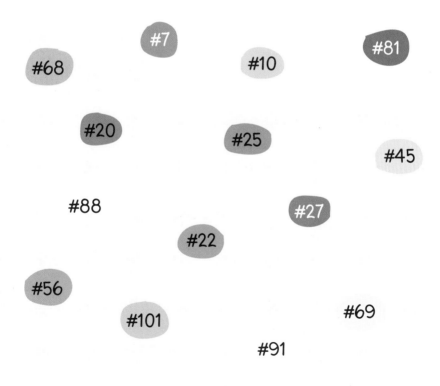

#7

#68

#10

#81

#20

#25

#45

#88

#27

#22

#56

#101

#69

#91

MUSIC

Music can change your mood!

You could try listening to:

- gently uplifting music when you're feeling sad, flat, stuck or unmotivated

- super upbeat dance music when you're feeling like you need to move some energy, dance and shake and lift yourself up

- calming music when you are anxious, angry or panicky

- chilled-out background music when you want to feel relaxed and focused

- sad music when you need to let go, cry and feel your feelings

- powerful music when you need a boost of confidence

- binaural beats when you're feeling anxious or you need a calmer, more focused state of mind.

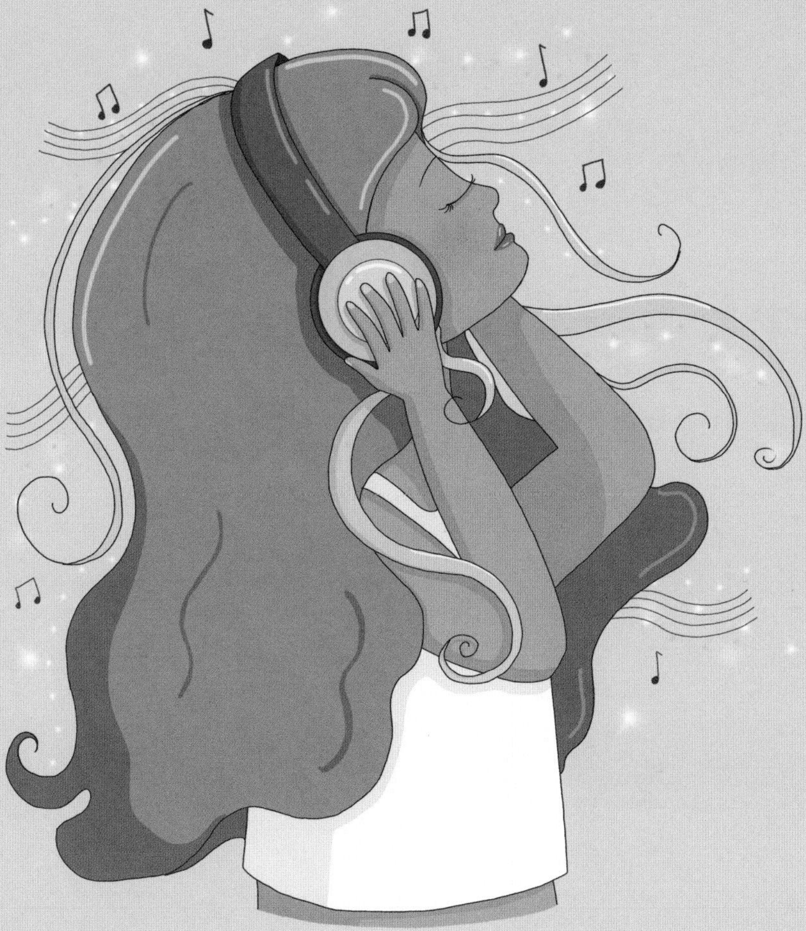

BODY TAPS

Body-tapping is a gentle practice to bring you back to your body when you're feeling spacey.

Gently pat, tap and stroke over your whole body. Tap lightly down each arm, pat down your chest and belly, stroke your fingers down your neck and so on.

You can avoid any areas that feel unsafe or triggering.

Pay attention to the sensations this creates in your body. Don't make it too repetitive and don't just go through the motions; stay in tune with the sensations in your fingertips and on your skin.

When you are finished, pause to feel any echoes: tingles, warmth, body (somatic) sensations, energy and emotions.

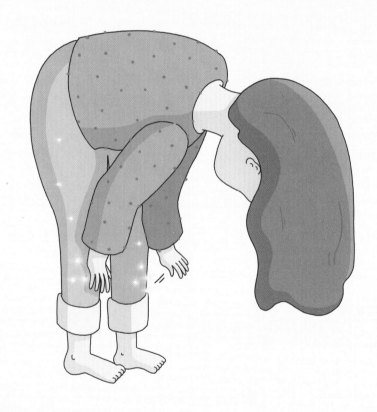

69

MINDFUL WALK

Go outside if you can (but do this around your house if you can't). Take a deep breath and begin walking.

- Notice the way your feet feel on the ground.

- Pay attention to the sounds around you.

- Become aware of light and shadows.

- Describe to yourself the physical sensations of walking. What do you notice in your body?

- Tune in to your breath.

- Notice if there is a breeze. Pay attention to the feeling of the air on your skin.

- Take note of any smells around you.

- Reach out and touch things. Seek out different textures and describe them to yourself.

If your mind wanders, gently acknowledge it and bring your attention back to the present moment, focusing on your senses. See if you can reach 5 minutes to start and increase the time when you feel comfortable.

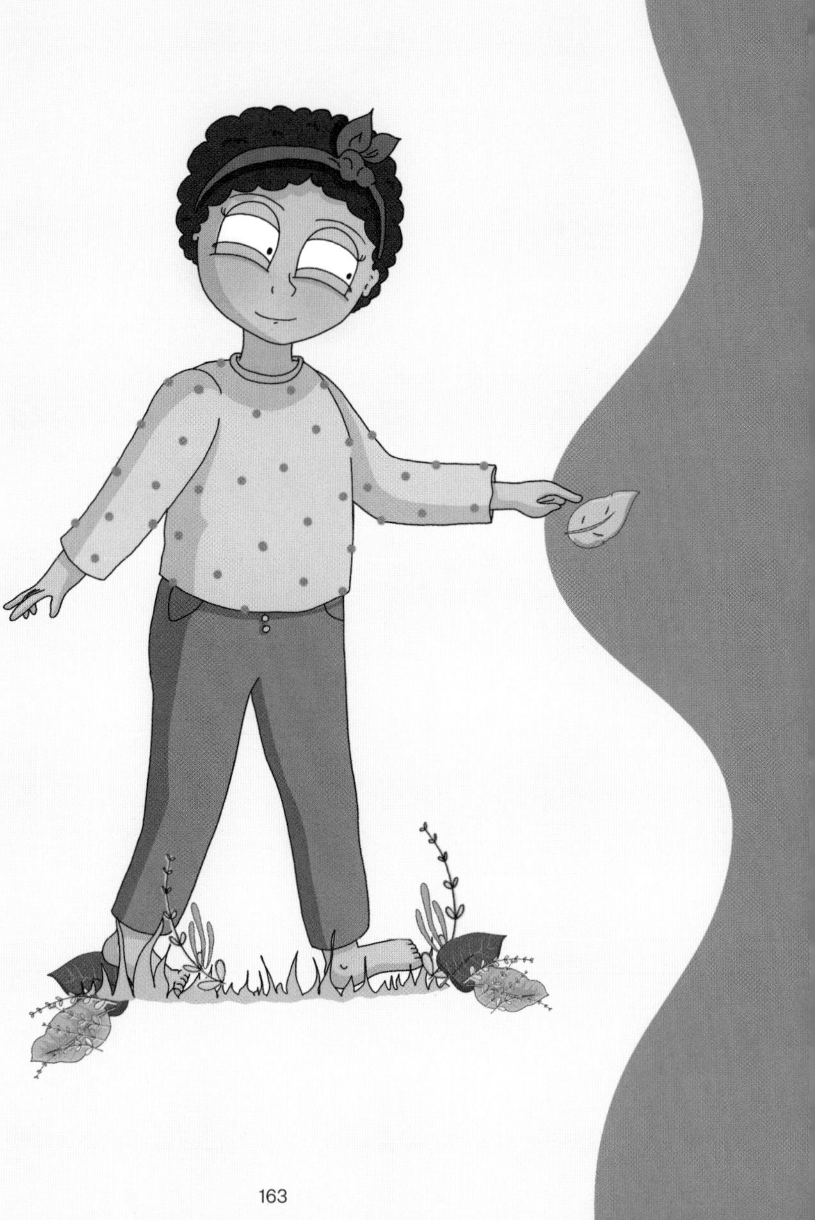

70

CANDLE CALM

Light a candle and dim or turn off the lights.
Focus all your attention on the candle.

Focus on slow deep breaths as you describe the experience of watching the candle:

✿ What does the flame look like?

✿ If the candle is scented, what can you smell?

✿ If you hover your hands closer to the flame, can you feel the warmth on your palms?

✿ Is the candlelight creating shadows in the room?

Take some time here to allow yourself to relax and focus on the present.

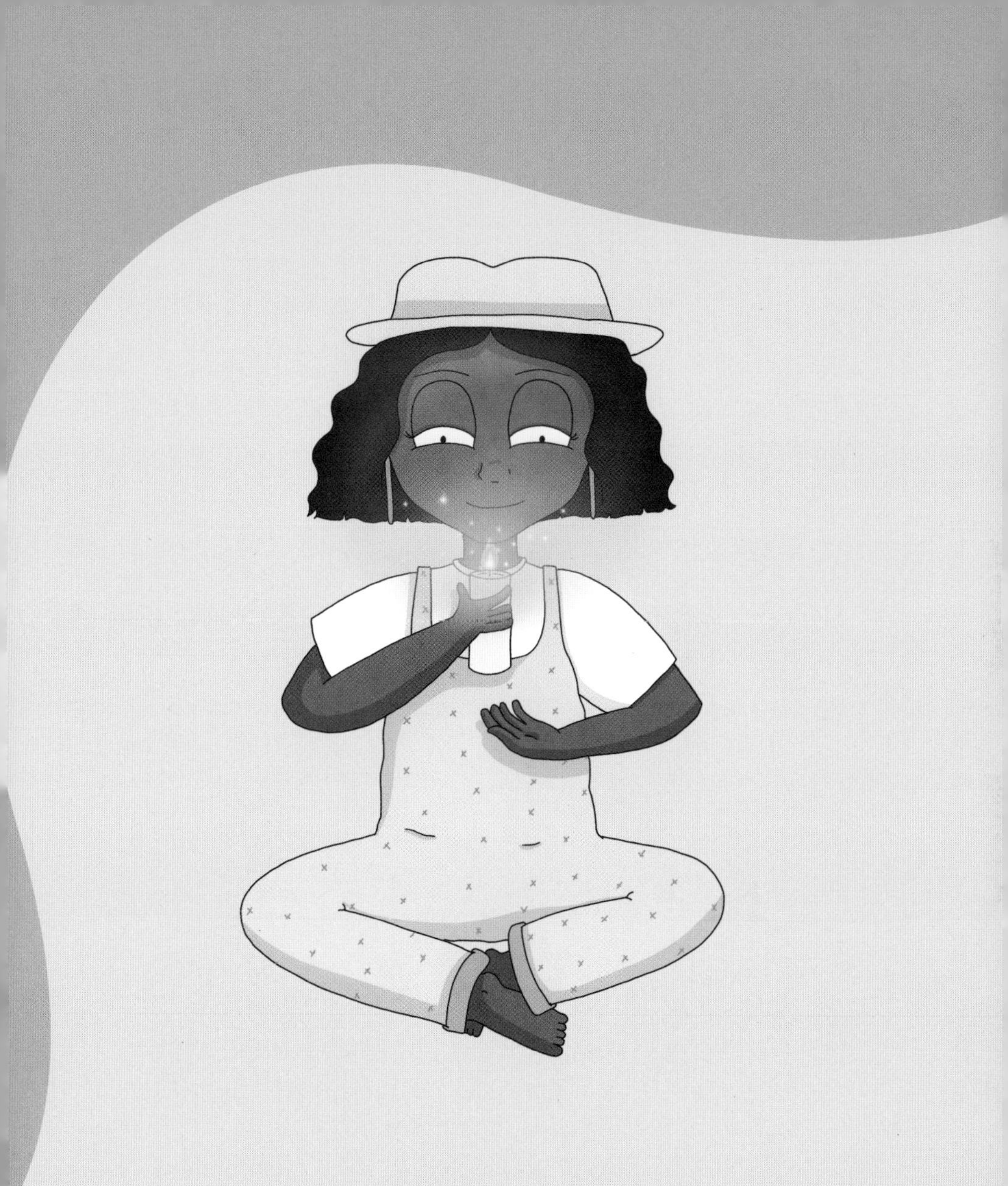

PRACTICE
MAKES
PROGRESS.

Don't beat yourself up
when things don't go
perfectly the first time,
or when you struggle to
build a new habit.

Remember: there are no
failures; only trial runs.

A little self-compassion,
patience and perseverance
goes a long way.

71

SELF-CHECK

Stop what you are doing and take a
moment to check in with yourself.

Ask yourself:

- ❀ How am I feeling right now?

- ❀ What am I thinking about?

- ❀ How do I feel physically in my body?

- ❀ Is there anything from yesterday or the past week that is still impacting me today? If yes, what can I do today to let go and become more present?

- ❀ How was my sleep last night? Have I eaten and drunk enough water? Have I moved my body?

- ❀ What is my intention for the day ahead?

- ❀ What predictions or assumptions am I making about the day ahead?

- ❀ What do I need to do today to support my wellbeing?

You can think about your answers or write them down.

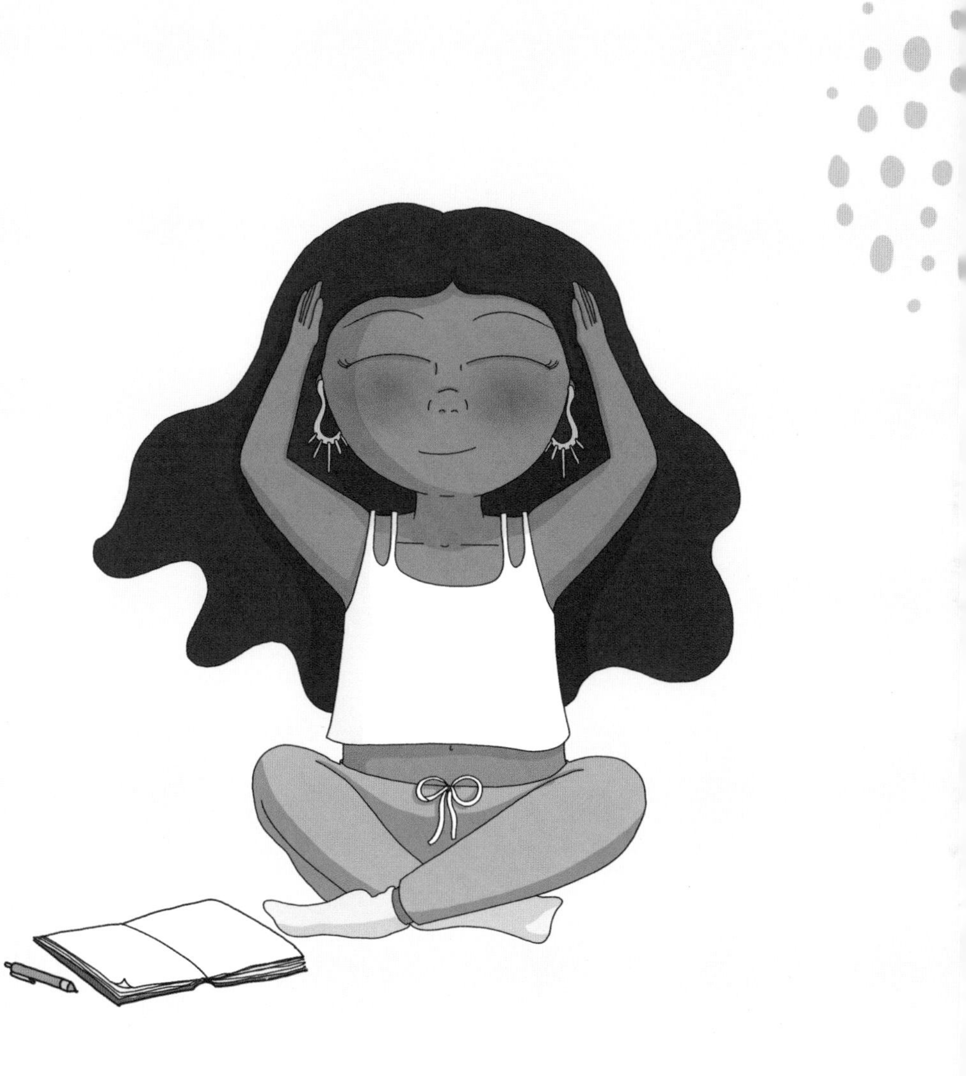

72

INNER CONNECTION

**This simple, soulful practice helps connect you
to your innate wisdom, intuition and needs.**

1. Place your hand on your heart and close your eyes if that feels okay, otherwise soften your gaze downwards. You might like to place your other hand over your belly, connecting with your 'gut feeling' and intuition.

2. Come into stillness. Your only movement is your breath. Notice your thoughts.

3. Observe the sensations under your hands as you tune in to your heart space and your belly.

4. When you have settled into your body, ask yourself, 'What do I need?' Sit and wait patiently, observing what comes up.

There's no right or wrong here. Don't force yourself into an answer. Just allow space and listen.

You may have a thought, urge, impulse or need that surfaces seemingly out of nowhere. Say to yourself, 'I see you, I hear you, I honour this need.' You might choose to go and meet that need, or you might like to come back to your breath again and ask, 'What else?'

It may take some practice before you notice an answer. Many people spend years of their lives disconnected from their own needs, shutting down their own desires and putting others above themselves. Over time this may have become a reflexive habit of people pleasing.

Your nervous system unconsciously does this to keep you safe; it isn't your fault.

Practices like this help to build a bridge back to your authentic self and to begin to hear and honour your needs.

73

FLOOR FOOT RUBS

Take off your shoes, sit on a chair and place both feet firmly on the floor. Begin to glide your feet back and forth along the ground. Make this movement slow and rhythmic. Focus on breathing deeply for at least a minute.

Notice:

- ✿ the feeling on the soles of your feet as they slide along the ground
- ✿ the sounds your feet make as they glide
- ✿ the sensations in your calves and legs
- ✿ the emotions this brings up
- ✿ the feeling on the soles of your feet when you come to a stop.

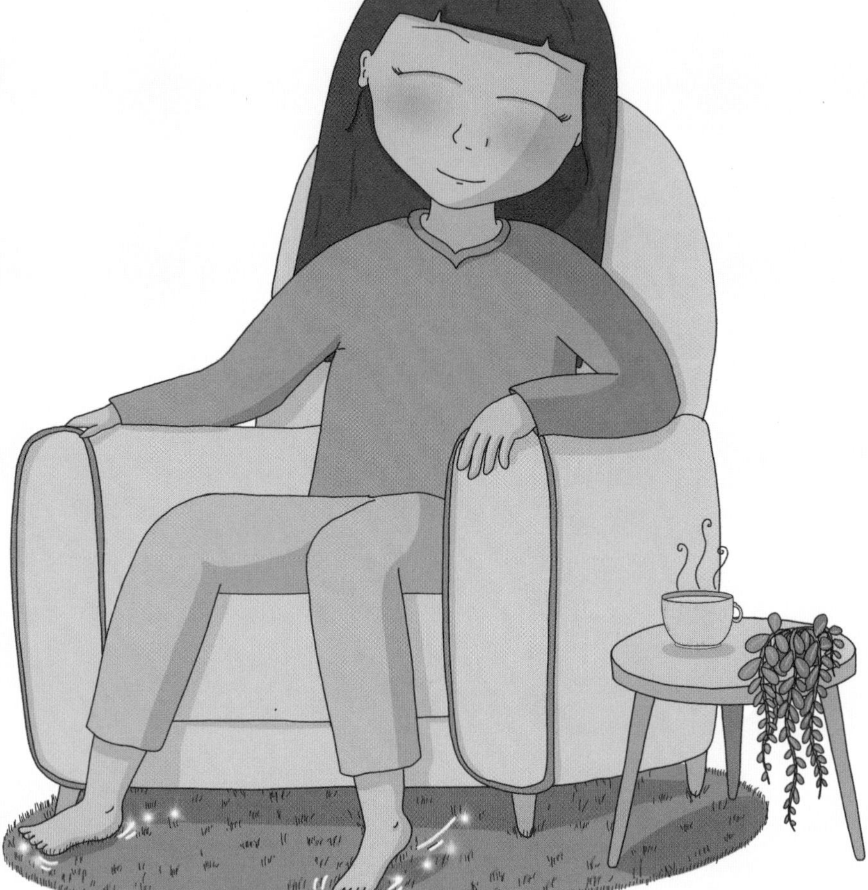

74

EYE REST

If you feel overwhelmed or overstimulated, this tool will calm you by reducing your sensory input.

Here's how:

1. Find a cosy spot to lie down where you won't be disturbed.

2. Cover your eyes with an eye mask or a weighted eye pillow. (A pillow case or small blanket will do.)

3. Rest your focus on your breath and the weighted feeling on your eyes.

4. Notice thoughts that surface and emotions that bubble up. Watch them come and go like clouds in the sky. Stay here for as long as you need.

75

HOT CHOCOLATE BREATH

This delightful breathing tool will help you to extend your exhale and restore some calm.

Here's how:

1. Imagine that you are holding a cup of hot chocolate in your hands. (You can imagine other things too, like a cup of tea, soup, your favourite winter stew or a hot coffee.)

2. As you slowly inhale through your nose, imagine you are breathing in the rich aroma of the chocolatey goodness.

3. Slowly exhale through pursed lips, as though you are trying to cool down the hot chocolate before taking a sip.

4. Repeat steps 1 to 3 for as long as you like. You could even imagine a gentle warming feeling in your hands as this lovely breathing technique soothes and relaxes you.

76

MANTRA BREATH

Pair these calming affirmations/mantras with your breath to find some comfort in your day. You could go through all of them, pick a handful of your favourites or use one pair on repeat.

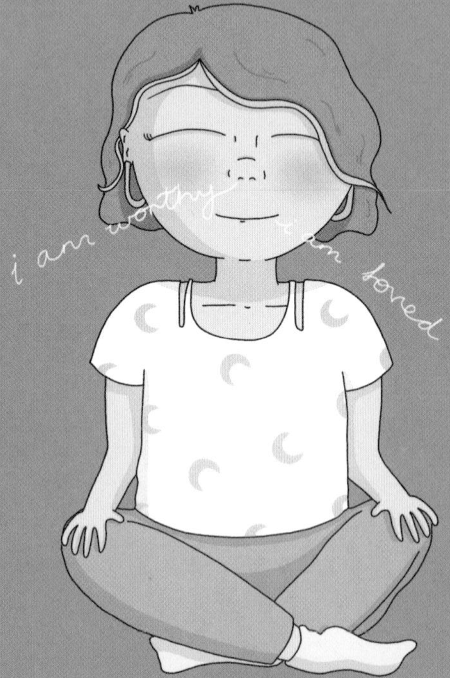
i am worthy
i am loved

Match your inhale and exhale with reading these phrases to yourself:

ON YOUR INHALE:

✿ My mind is relaxed

✿ Breathe in calm

✿ Relaxing

✿ Absorbing safety

✿ Inviting stillness

✿ Creating space

✿ I welcome expansion

✿ Inhaling the courage to be with my experience

✿ Inhaling nourishment and renewal

✿ I am safe

✿ Inhaling acceptance

ON YOUR EXHALE:

✿ My body is relaxed

✿ Breathe out tension

✿ Letting go

✿ Dissolving any need for armouring

✿ Releasing any need for rushing

✿ Melt and unwind

✿ I allow my body to soften

✿ Exhaling anything holding me back

✿ Exhaling stagnation and stuckness

✿ I am secure

✿ Exhaling and letting go of judgement

77

PHOTOGRAPHY WALK

Ground yourself in the present while training your brain to focus on life's beautiful details and glimmering moments.

Here's how:

1. Take a walk and have your phone/camera ready. You could walk outside, or even just around the room.

2. Take close-up pictures of little details you notice, such as fabric, insects, flowers or plants. See if you can notice any interesting textures, light, shadows or angles.

3. Immerse yourself in the present by using your phone/camera to bring your focus back to the details around you and your senses.

4. If you don't have a phone/camera, you can still focus on all the little details in your surroundings that you find interesting.

78

MiNDFUL BiTE

Most of the time we eat on the run or on autopilot.
And while eating mindfully for an entire meal
would be a great thing to strive for, starting with
a mindful first bite is the perfect first step.

It's simple. Right before you take the first bite of a meal, pause:

- ❀ What smells do you notice?
- ❀ What colours and textures can you see in your food? ·
- ❀ How does the food feel in your hand? Or how does the fork feel between your fingers?
- ❀ Take a bite and hold the food in your mouth for a moment. What is the texture? Taste? Temperature?
- ❀ Slowly chew and swallow the food, continuing to describe the sensory experience.

Now you're free to eat the rest of your meal however you like!

HiNT: If you're feeling anxious, chewing gum, sucking sour candy, eating strong mints or sipping water can help you feel calm again.

79

SINGLE FOCUS

Pick a random object on which to fix your focus.
Pour all of your attention into this object.

Describe to yourself:

🌼 all its tiny details such as colours, shape, texture . . .

🌼 the way it feels in your hands, its weight

🌼 the way the light hits it and where its shadows fall.

Each time you notice your mind wandering, you get lost
in thought or you lose focus, gently bring your attention
back to the object with compassion and non-judgement.

Set a timer and try this for 1 minute. You can extend this
time as you get more practice.

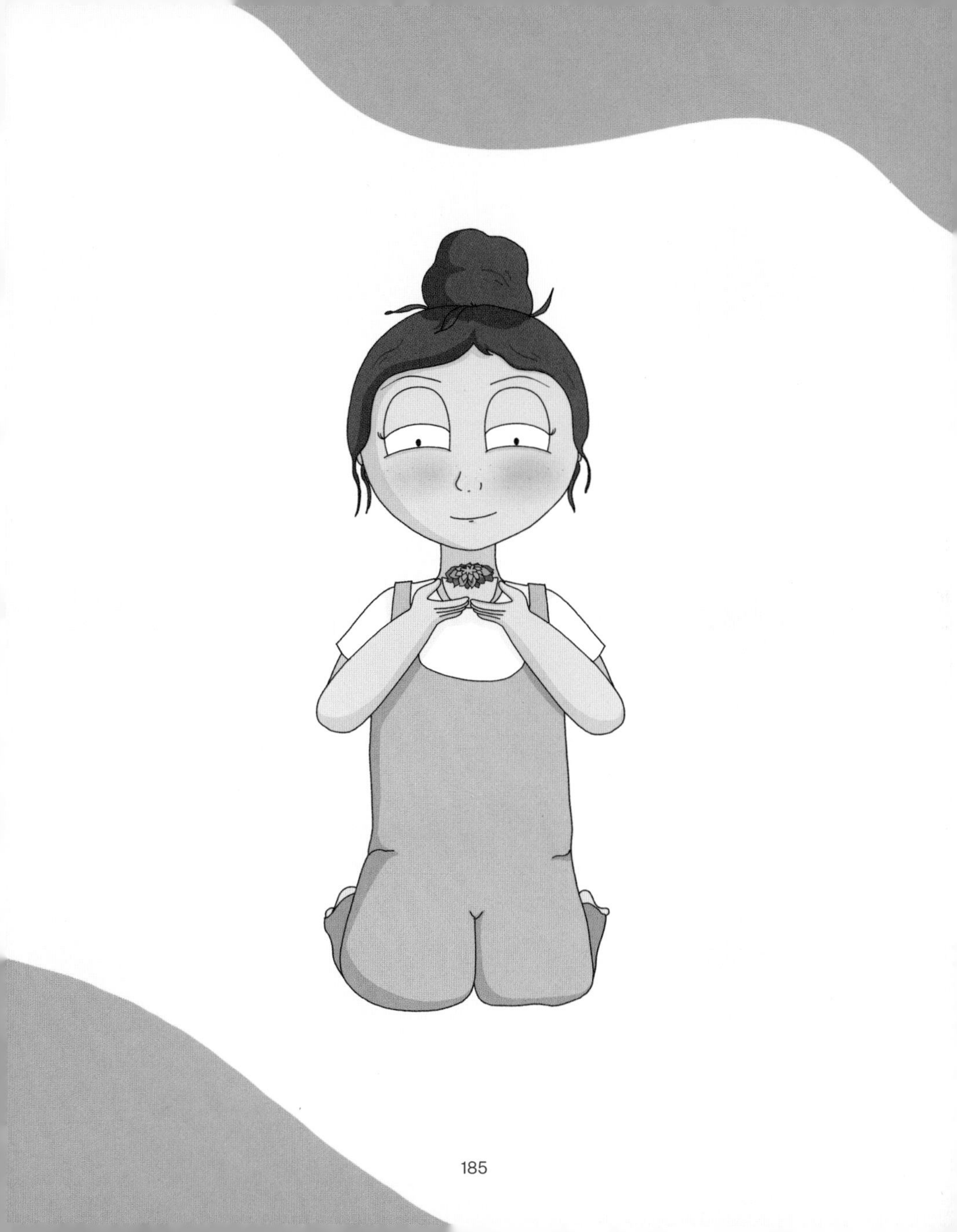

80

COPING STATEMENTS

Read and repeat as needed:

- Not everything I think is true.

- This feeling will pass.

- I have survived every hard thing I have ever been through.

- I am stronger than I give myself credit for.

- I do not need to fight or fix my feelings.

- Distress reminds me to come back to my breath.

- My emotions are messengers signalling to me my needs.

- I choose to honour my emotions by allowing them space.

- I listen to the wisdom of my body and trust in my innate ability to heal and flourish.

- I enrich my soul by speaking to myself with kindness and compassion.

- I take each day as it comes, one step at a time.

- A bad day does not equal a bad life.

Think of some of your own self-soothing statements and read them whenever you need to ground your mind.

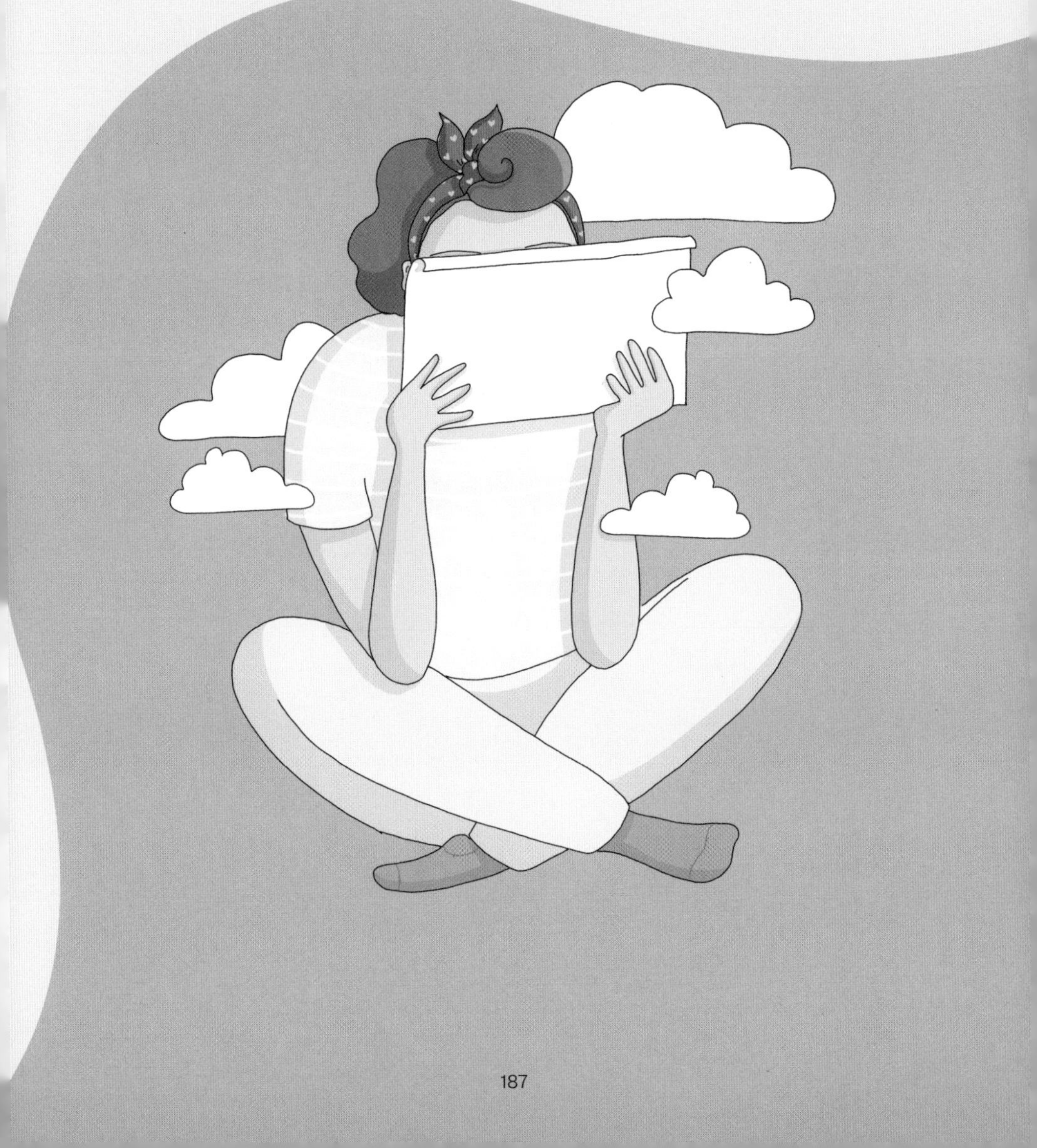

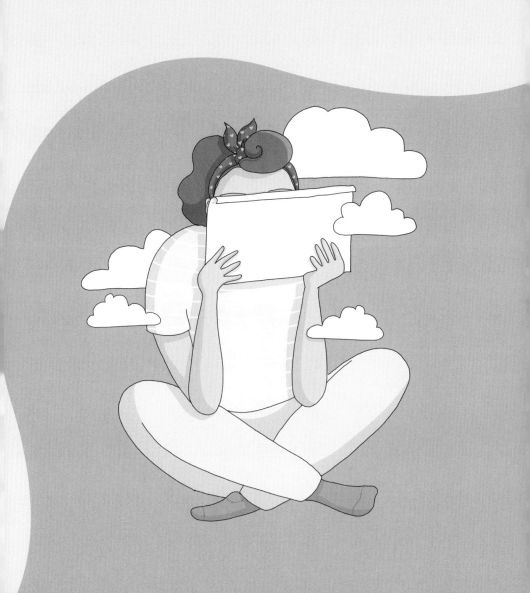

YOU CAN'T ALWAYS
THINK OR TALK YOUR
WAY TO HEALING.

COMMUNICATING
VIA THE BODY IS THE
LANGUAGE OF SOOTHING
AND HEALING THE
NERVOUS SYSTEM.

81

COMFORT COLOUR

Pick a colour to be your grounding colour; representing safety, comfort and inner peace.

When you need a calming anchor, bring your colour to mind. Close your eyes and breathe slowly. Imagine this colour filling you up and wrapping a sense of calm and safety around you.

When you're ready, open your eyes and begin to slowly scan the room. Notice anything you see in your grounding colour, reminding you of a feeling of safety both within you and surrounding you.

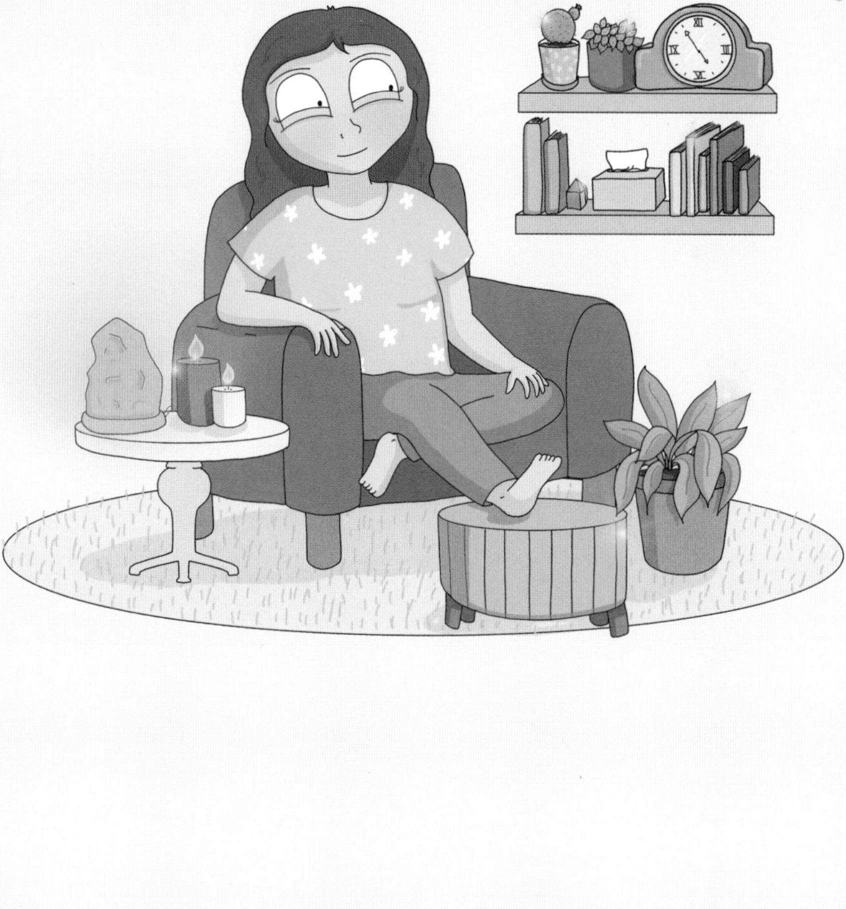

82

COMFORTING TOUCH

Choose an object that feels soothing and
calming, such as a crystal, a stone, a small piece
of fabric, a button, a coin, a small toy . . .

This will be your grounding object, to carry with you in your bag or pocket for support if you feel anxious or overwhelmed.

Start by 'imprinting' your intentions for this object.

Hold it in your hand and observe it with a soft focus while breathing deeply.

In your mind offer words of safety and calm to this object. For example, you might think, 'When I hold you I am calm and grounded in the present. You remind me to connect with my breath, to slow my mind and to trust that the tricky times will pass.'

You might like to imagine a protective light surrounding and infusing the object.

Then, whenever you feel distressed you can hold your grounding object, reminding yourself of its intentions. 'I am safe. This will pass. Breathe.'

83

BODY CONTACT

Come home to your body with this grounding tool.

Here's how:

1. First, drop into your breath; observing your inhale and exhale and perhaps invite them to settle and slow.

2. Now, with your eyes shut or your focus soft and your gaze down, begin to tune in to your body.

3. Notice the contact points of your body with the surface(s) beneath you.

4. Notice the contact points of your body with other parts of your body.

5. Notice the contact points of your clothes against your body.

Afterwards, reflect on what it was like to take a moment to be grounded and present in your body.

84

ANCHOR

Anchoring yourself to the present is helpful if you
find yourself feeling triggered, spacey, dissociative,
or overwhelmed by future worries and fears.

Fill in the blanks and repeat gently to yourself:

✿ I am here

✿ I am _____
(describe where you are specifically, e.g. 'in my kitchen')

✿ I'm in _____
(state the city/town you're in)

✿ It's _____ (day of the week) at _____(specific time)

✿ It's _____ (describe the weather outside, e.g. 'sunny',
'raining')

✿ I can feel my _____ (describe
one body contact point, e.g. 'feet on the floor', 'hair brushing my neck')

✿ I can hear _____
(name a few things you can hear)

✿ I can see _____
(name the first thing that catches your attention)

✿ And I am safe here in this moment.

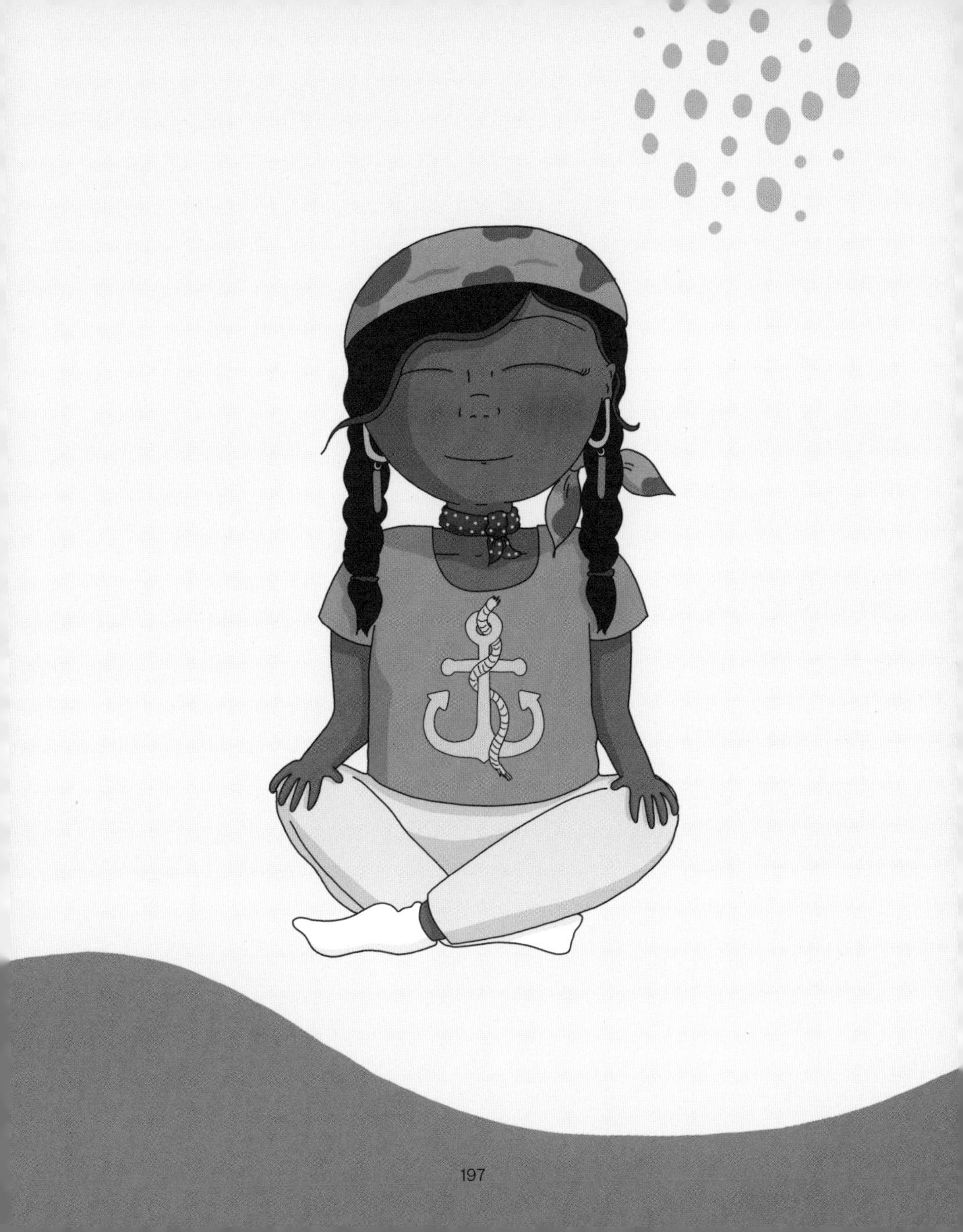

85

HEAT

**Sometimes you need a little warmth
to feel cosy, safe and calm.**

Here are a few things to try:

- Rest a heated wheat bag on your belly or chest.

- Snuggle up with a hot-water bottle.

- Immerse yourself in some warm water (a bath, spa or shower).

- Spend some time in a sauna.

- Make yourself a cuppa and relish the feeling of the warm mug in your hands.

- Wrap up in a cosy blanket.

- Sit by a fire in winter.

- Rub your hands back and forth quickly to generate heat in your palms and fingers then cup your palms gently over your closed eyes and forehead.

86

SOOTHiNG WATER

Run yourself a nice hot bath or take a long, hot shower. You can also fill up a large bowl with hot water and make it a hand or foot bath.

Take your time to savour the sensations of the water against your skin.

Close your eyes and describe the experience using all of your senses.

You can add other sensory elements to the environment to amplify the soothing experience, such as:

- bath bombs
- bubbles
- nice-smelling body wash
- a lit candle

- relaxing music
- an exfoliating glove
- essential oils
- a face mask.

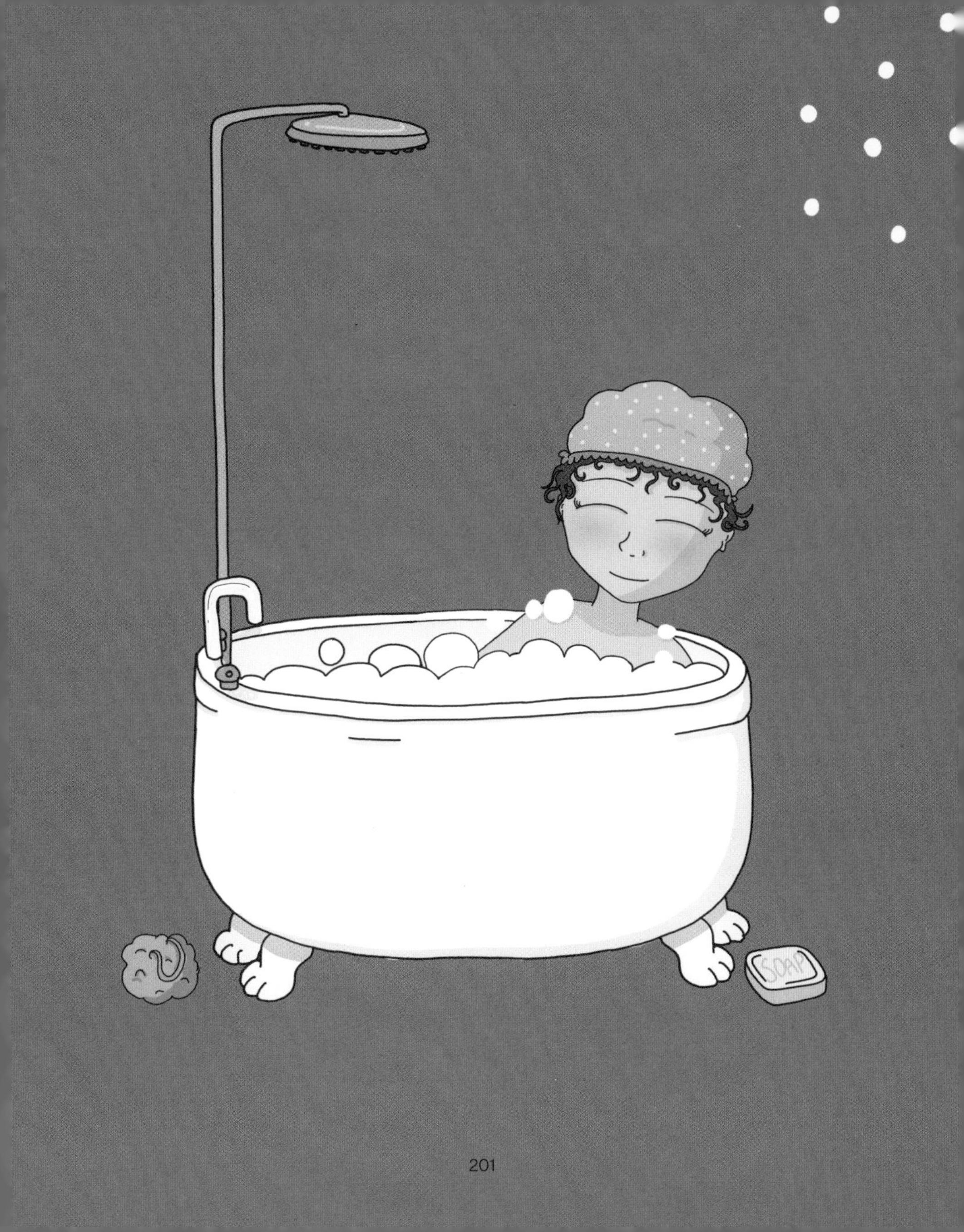
SOAP

87

SOOTHING SOUNDS

Soothe yourself with your favourite sounds.

Pick a sound from the list below (or a favourite of your own), search for it on a Spotify or YouTube playlist, then grab a cosy spot, close your eyes, and spend 5–20 minutes focusing on the sounds and your breath.

- ❀ ocean waves
- ❀ binaural beats
- ❀ raindrops on the roof
- ❀ classical music
- ❀ nature sounds such as birdsong
- ❀ relaxing piano music
- ❀ thunder
- ❀ bubbling stream
- ❀ wind
- ❀ white noise.

This tool combines nicely with tools like #17, #19, #21, #27, #32, #62, #70 or #85.

88

GAZE AND SWEEP

This tool draws on gentle comforting touch while
helping you feel grounded and calm by combining
bilateral stimulation and vagal nerve stimulation.

Here's how:

1. Lie on your back or take a comfortable seat.

2. Stroke your hands, one after the other, over your chest
   with your head facing straight ahead and your eyes gazing
   over to your far left. Continue for 30–60 seconds.

3. Cross your arms over your chest and sweep your hands
   down opposite arms from your shoulders all the way to
   your hands. Repeat as you gaze your eyes to your far
   right. Continue for 30–60 seconds.

If this doesn't feel good for your eyes you can close them and
just stick to the gentle stroking movements.

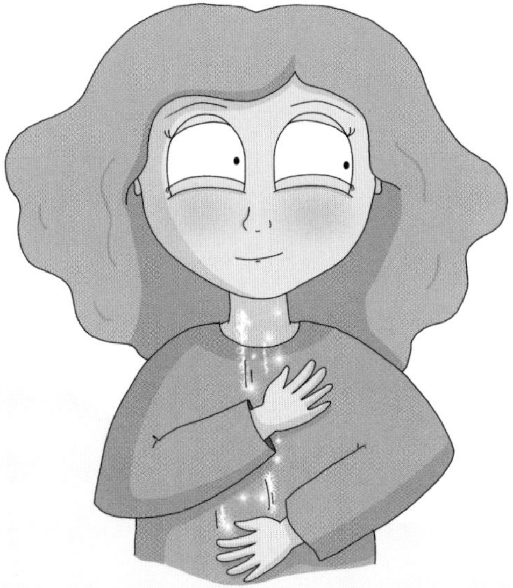

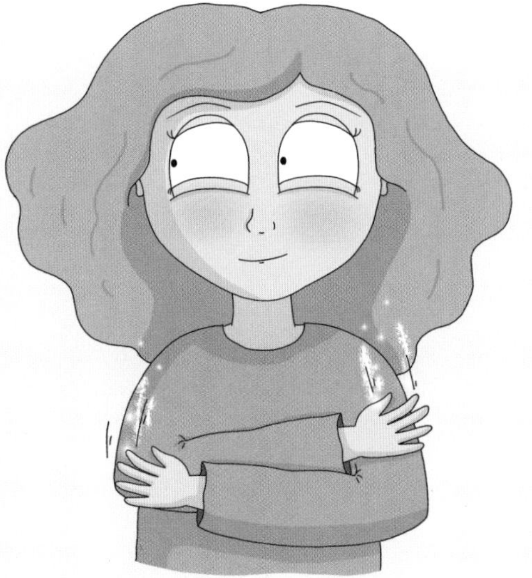

89

THE BURN LIST

Write down on paper any things that are no longer serving you or that you are ready to let go of and release, then (safely!) burn the paper. Imagine whatever is written being cleared away by the flames, a weight lifting from you as it is set free into smoke.

Ideas to write about for release:

* things that are worrying you that are outside your control to change

* a letter to things or people to whom you feel anger or resentment

* old habits you are ready to move on from

* limiting beliefs or fears that are no longer serving you

* a letter to someone you're not able to speak to, voicing what you wish you could say.

* a letter to a past version of yourself offering words you needed to hear at the time.

* guilt or regrets you are holding on to that you are ready to release.

ROCKING RELEASE

Rocking is deeply soothing to the nervous system. Think of the way we instinctually rock when holding a baby, or the way we might shake, rock or sway when we're upset or in shock. Intentional rocking can safely release our emotions, tension and anxiety.

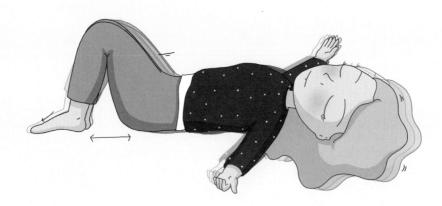

Here's how:

1. Lie down. Plant your feet on the ground with your knees pointed to the ceiling.

2. Gently and rhythmically pulse your feet into the floor so that your body begins to rock back and forth. Use as little effort as possible. This should feel soothing, not 'trancey' or spacey.

3. Continue for 1–5 minutes before coming to stillness. Notice how you feel.

CUT YOURSELF SOME SLACK, MY LOVE. YOU WOULDN'T TALK LIKE THAT TO A FRIEND.

TREAT YOURSELF THE WAY YOU WOULD TREAT A SMALL CHILD.

* Nourish your body when you are hungry

* Tuck yourself into bed for an early night when you are tired

* Wrap your arms compassionately around yourself or reach out to a loved one when you need comfort

* Allow yourself to feel and express your emotions

SUPPORT CREW

This is a beautiful visualisation tool that creates your very own support crew.

Here's how:

1. Close your eyes and sink into your breath.

2. You're going to bring to mind three people. They could be someone you know, a fictional character, someone you admire who you've never met or even an animal.

3. Bring to mind someone who represents strength.

4. Bring to mind someone who represents wisdom.

5. Bring to mind someone who represents love, unconditional caring and support.

6. Spend some time imagining these people with you, standing around you with a hand on your shoulder. Think about what each of them would say to you. What words of support would they offer?

These people are your support crew. Whenever you need guidance you can close your eyes, visualise your crew and ask them for some words of strength, wisdom and love.

92

TURNING INWARDS AND OPENING YOUR HEART

Find introspection and emotional release
while fostering a sense of calm with a caterpillar
pose. Then find confidence, openness
and self-expression with a fish pose.

First, turn inwards with a 'caterpillar' pose. From seated,
extend your legs and fold forward over them. Allow your
muscles to relax by propping a pillow between your legs
and head for support.

Spend 1–5 minutes here, feeling your belly expand into
your legs or the pillow beneath you.

Next, create some space and expansion with a heart-
opening pose like a 'fish' pose. You can use supports under
your head and under your back between your shoulder
blades. Your arms can be out wide or by your sides as you
take beautiful deep breaths, feeling your chest and ribs
become spacious. Spend 1–5 minutes here too.

93

EMOTIONAL PROCESSING AND RELEASE

Use this tool to move between a tricky emotion and a sense of grounding and safety. This teaches you that you can safely tolerate and process uncomfortable feelings.

Here's how:

1. When you notice a tricky emotion (especially one that you would prefer to resist or push away) press pause and come to a comfy spot. Sit with your emotion for a minute or so, just observing it. Notice where you feel it in your body. Describe the emotion to yourself: its quality, size, shape and colour.

2. Then, come to standing. Move around, reaching out and touching different objects. Immerse yourself in your senses, describing textures, colours, lighting, temperatures, weights, smells, sounds and the feeling of objects under your fingers. Imagine you have never been here or seen these objects before. Spend at least a minute here.

3. Repeat the steps 1 and 2 above three to five times or until you feel your emotion softening, dissolving or releasing. This is a sign that you are processing and integrating it.

You can also use this tool to process a tricky memory; moving between playing the memory in your mind like a video and then grounding into your space.

94

ADRENAL HUG

Your adrenals are two small glands that sit above your kidneys. They release stress hormones (cortisol and adrenaline) when your sympathetic nervous system is activated under stress. For some people these glands work overtime and can become tired.

Here's how:

1. Let's send them some love. Rub your hands together back and forth as though you are warming them over a campfire. Create some heat, then bring your hands behind you to place them over your adrenal glands, like a warm hug.

2. Close your eyes and imagine sending your breath into the space beneath your hands, sending some love to these hard-working wee poppets.

3. Come back to stillness. Bring one hand to your belly and the other to your chest, and witness your emotions, your body sensations and your thoughts. Be curious about any changes you feel and breathe deeply to come back to calm.

95

DUAL AWARENESS

Practising holding two points of focus at the same time
will help you to be able to feel distressing emotions
while remaining grounded and able to cope.

Here's how:

1. Ask yourself 'What has my attention right now?' If your thoughts have your attention, can you notice what sensations are in your body?

2. Now look around your space. Notice colours and textures. Notice where your eyes are drawn to. What object do they want to land on? Stay with that object and soak it in.

3. Come back to your body. What are you aware of now? Wiggle your fingers and toes. Do you get a sense of warmth? Notice your breath and your heartbeat. Keep your eyes open and bring your attention to your chosen object. Hold your focus on your body as well as the object.

4. Notice if anything changes and shifts in your body. Don't force anything; just observe.

5. Allow your body to move if it wants to; perhaps moving your head, swaying, stretching, twisting . . . Try to move mindfully and slowly, almost as if you are moving through water.

6. Slowly come back to stillness and ask yourself again 'What has my attention right now?'

There is no right or wrong outcome. This practice simply builds your capacity to be in your body and present in your life at the same time.

96

THE BOILING BREATHER

Every time you boil the jug for a cuppa, rather than scrolling on your phone or rushing off to do something else, stand by the jug with one hand on your chest and the other hand on your belly and breathe deeply and slowly.

Stay here until the jug has boiled, breathing and listening to the sound of the bubbling water.

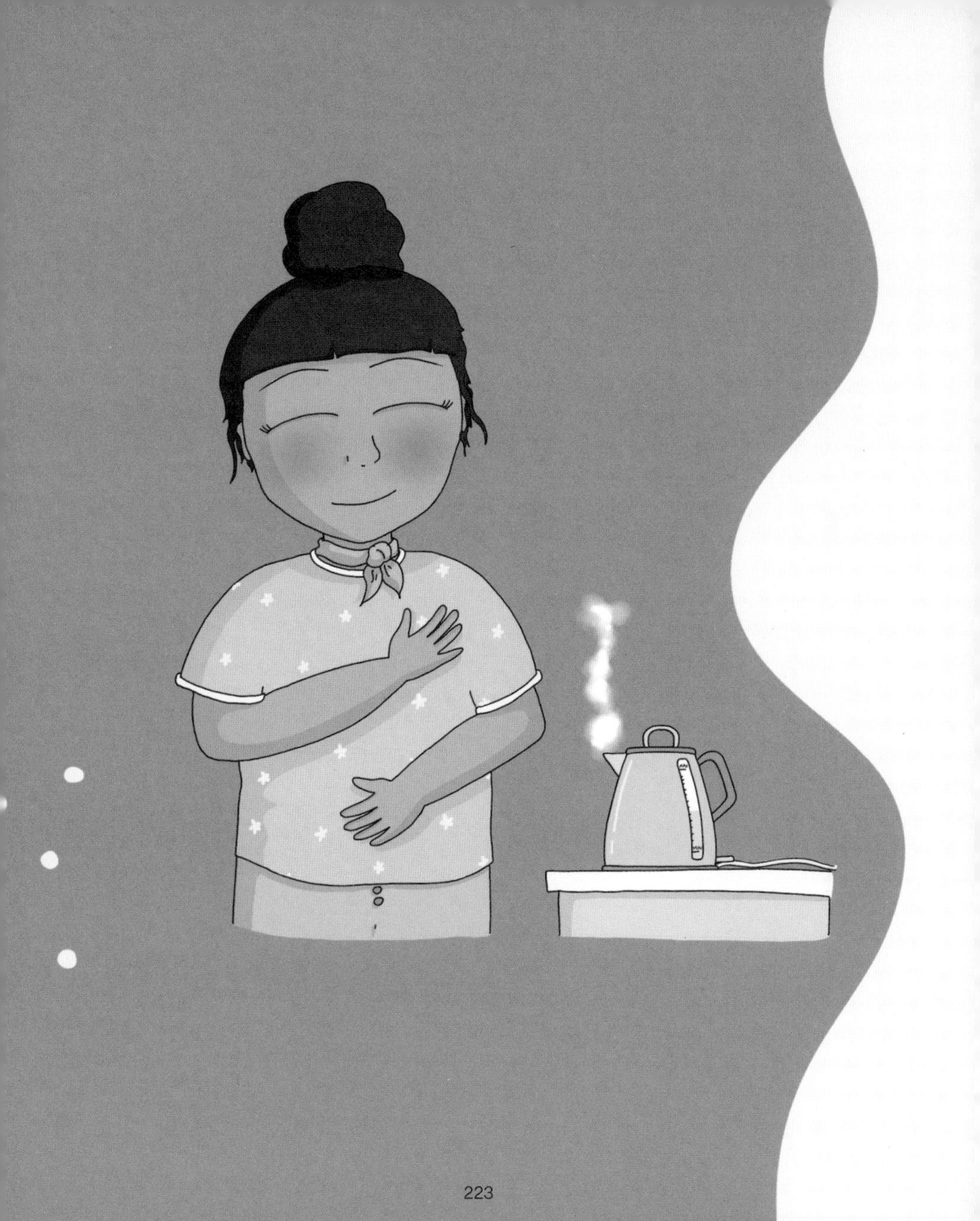

97

WAVE BREATHING

In this three-part breathing practice you'll inhale like a wave: filling up your belly first, then your side ribs, then your lungs and chest. Your exhale can either happen in reverse or, if this is a bit tricky, you can sigh out your exhale as one breath.

Here's how:

1. Breathe in through your nose, directing your inhale down to your diaphragm so your belly expands.

2. Move your inhale to the sides of your ribs, feeling your ribcage gently flare open.

3. Allow your inhale to travel upwards, expanding your upper chest.

4. Exhale in reverse (chest, side ribs, belly) or all at once.

5. Continue wave breathing for 1–5 minutes.

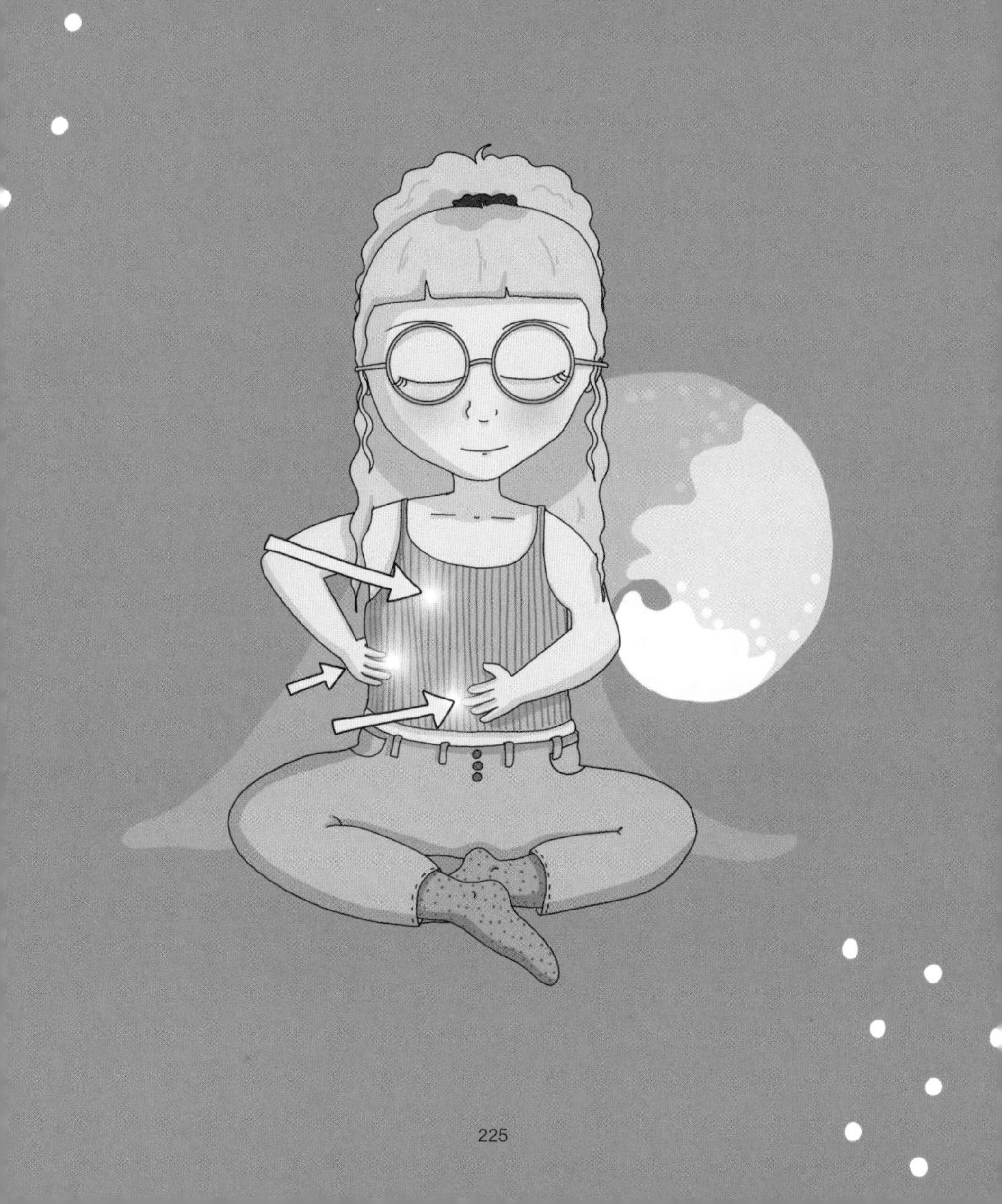

BiAS

Your brain is designed to look for negatives
and danger in the world (negativity bias)
and to seek evidence of things you already
believe to be true (confirmation bias).

Try this:

1. Look around the room for 30 seconds and make a
   mental note of all the green things you see. Do this
   now before you read ahead any further.

2. List all the blue things you saw. Yes, blue.

What happened? Chances are this threw you a little. You were only looking for green things!

This is an example of how negativity bias and confirmation bias works.

A negativity bias is when your brain looks for things that could go wrong (to keep you safe of course). This is a survival instinct that can make you feel rather glum.

A confirmation bias looks for evidence to prove something you already believe to be true. If you believe people are good and trustworthy, you will see that in the world. If you believe 'I never stick to anything' or 'I'm not worthy' or 'I'm always getting things wrong', your brain will see that instead.

These biases actively filter out things that don't agree with them. Your brain filtered out all the colours other than green, right? Bias alters your perception of the world.

Biases can become self-fulfilling prophecies. If you believe you never stick to anything, chances are you'll end up self-sabotaging by giving up, which further proves the belief.

Next time you find yourself 'down the rabbit hole' in your thinking, remember this exercise. Perhaps you can make a conscious effort to notice some glimmering moments too.

99

MIRROR MANTRAS

We are often at our most critical in front of the mirror, pointing out all our perceived flaws and picking at ourselves. Hello, inner critic!

This can become a habit. Let's do something about that!

Write some lovely mantras, affirmations or reminders for yourself on some Post-It Notes and pop them up on your mirror.

Some ideas of what to write:

✿ I commit to speaking kindly to myself and about my body.

✿ I am worthy, just the way I am.

✿ My body is the vessel for my spirit. While I'm not defined by my body, it deserves to be treated well.

✿ I am worthy, loveable and deserving of compassion.

✿ I am grateful to my body for . . .

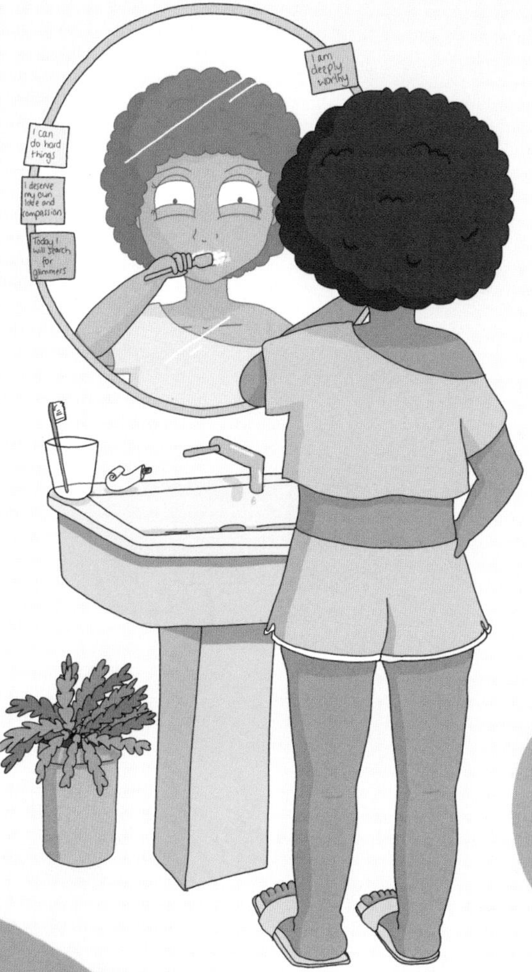
I am deeply worthy
I can do hard things
I deserve my own love and compassion
Today I will search for glimmers

Place one hand against the mirror, as though you were touching your hand, and repeat a mantra or two.

100

LOVING KINDNESS

Place your hands over your heart. Breathe into
your heart space and say to yourself: 'May I
be safe, may I be well, may I be at peace.'

Try to extend this loving kindness to others:

❀ Think about someone you love. Imagine a bubble of
light around yourself and extending it to wrap around
the other person. Say to yourself: 'May they be safe,
may they be well, may they be at peace.'

❀ Think about someone you are having a hard time with
right now and do the same.

❀ Think about a group of people, like a community, or all
beings in the world. Say to yourself: 'May we be safe,
may we be well, may we be at peace'.

101

BREATH OF JOY

Use this breathing tool when your energy, mood and motivation are low. It can feel more uplifting than a cup of coffee!

Here's how:

1. Stand up. Inhale a third of your lung capacity as you swing your arms in front of you to shoulder height. Imagine filling your belly.

2. Inhale the next third as you swing your arms down then out to the side to shoulder height. Imagine filling your mid-ribs.

3. Inhale the final third of your breath as you swing your arms down and then all the way up over your head. Imagine filling your chest. These three steps are done quickly in a row.

4. Exhale in one big sigh (like a 'ha' sound) as you bend at the hips, swinging your upper body towards the floor; your knees bent and your arms out behind you.

5. Repeat five to ten times.

You can do this seated in a chair if preferred.

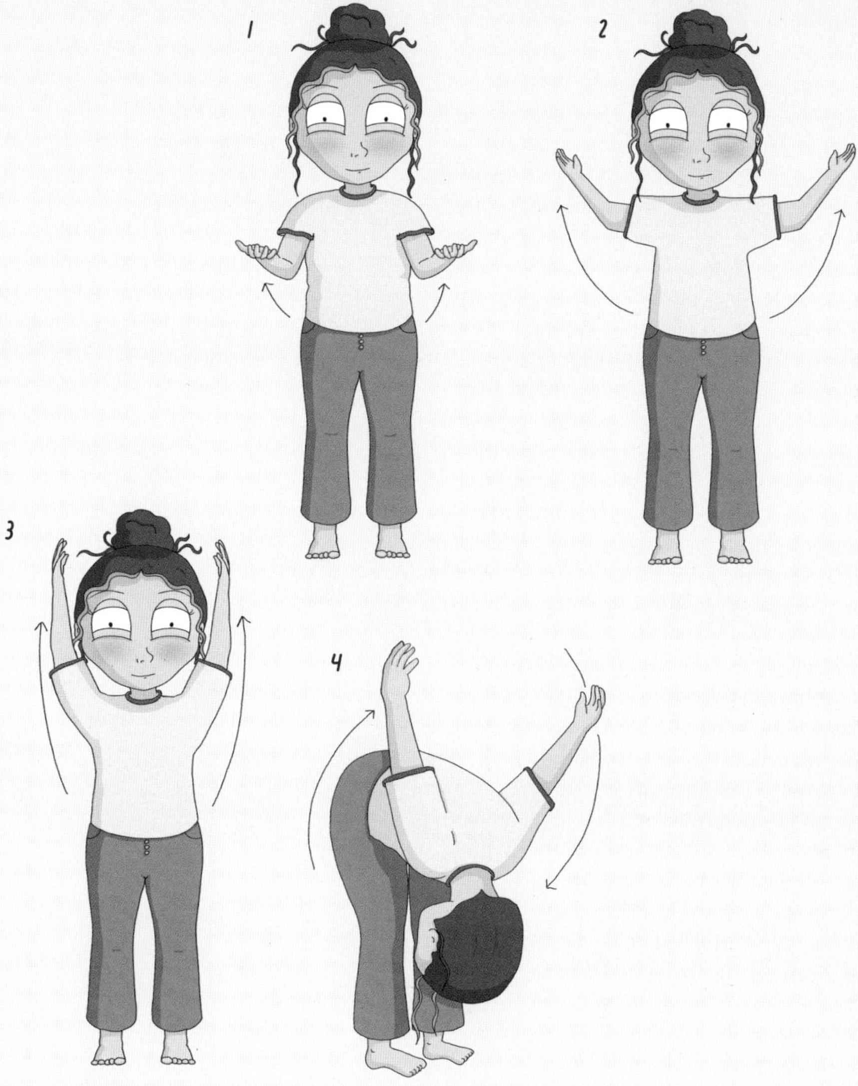
1
2
3
4

A HEALTHY NERVOUS
SYSTEM DOESN'T HAVE
TO ALWAYS BE CALM . . .

It's normal to experience
the full spectrum of
human emotions.

A healthy nervous system
is able to tolerate tricky
emotions & has the tools
to find its way back
to balance.

IDEAS FOR DAILY PRACTICE

It's a great idea to practise some calming tools every day.

Remember, we have to practise in the calm to access in the chaos.

By practising tools daily, you are rewiring your brain and nervous system. You are literally redesigning your life for calm, connection and compassion.

Here are a few combos that you might like to try (or build your own with your favourite tools). This list can also point you towards individual tools that support specific emotions and struggles.

For improving low mood:

COMBO 1: #7, #66, #85, #88, #100
COMBO 2: #8, #27, #58, #69
COMBO 3: #22, #32, #52, #91, #99
COMBO 4: #56, #67, #68, #86

For calming anxiety:

COMBO 1: #3, #14, #59, #87
COMBO 2: #11, #15, #61, #94, #97
COMBO 3: #5, #29, #34, #50
COMBO 4: #10, #17, #58, #80

For soothing stress:

COMBO 1: #5, #16, #22, #96
COMBO 2: #12, #37, #76
COMBO 3: #19, #42, #54, #65
COMBO 4: #26, #33, #51, #69

For easing anger:

COMBO 1: #4, #14, #44, #57
COMBO 2: #8, #49, #89, #93, #100
COMBO 3: #23, #47, #48, #61, #65

For building body positivity:

COMBO 1: #1, #35, #43, #91
COMBO 2: #9, #32, #64, #98
COMBO 3: #72, #89, #92, #100
COMBO 4: #12, #33, #51, #94, #99

For easing body discomfort and pain:

COMBO 1: #1, #37, #42, #76
COMBO 2: #5, 85, #87
COMBO 3: #19, #95, #98
COMBO 4: #36, #61, #100

For creating boundaries and dropping people-pleasing:

COMBO 1: #8, #48, #93
COMBO 2: #35, #51, #89
COMBO 3: #41, #49, #72, #91

For dissociation and disconnection:

COMBO 1: #4, #18, #55, #81
COMBO 2: #2, #13, #43, #56, #77
COMBO 3: #25, #68, #79, #84
COMBO 4: #32, #45, #50, #62, #83

USEFUL TERMS

🌸 **AMYGDALA** Your amygdala is the part of your brain that is responsible for emotional processing and emotional memory. It assesses whether something is threatening and sends an alarm to your body to alert you to danger. The amygdala is associated with anxiety and reflexive threat/trauma responses. If you have been through a lot of stress or trauma in your life, your amygdala can become hypervigilant, prone to activating your threat responses, even when they aren't needed.

🌸 **DORSAL VAGAL** The oldest and most primitive threat response state is driven by the dorsal vagal branch of your parasympathetic nervous system. This is also referred to as 'freeze or shut down'. A dorsal vagal state has layers ranging from feeling stuck, unmotivated, depressed, ashamed and dissociated to full immobility and collapse. This is a state of hypoarousal.

🌸 **DOWN REGULATE** Calming the limbic system and bringing your nervous system back to a place of balance. We use down-regulation techniques when your nervous system is hyperaroused/in a sympathetic state to help you discharge a threat response and feel calmer and more balanced.

🌸 **DYSREGULATION** Being in a state where your emotions or threat responses overwhelm your resources, capacity and ability to cope. This might look like being in a fight, flight, freeze or fawn state (see note on page 240) and can show up in your emotions, thinking styles and behaviours.

🌸 **HYPERAROUSAL** A feeling of being on high alert and in an overactive fight/flight response. Feeling angry, anxious, irritable, hypervigilant or easily startled.

HYPOAROUSAL Feeling shutdown in response to stress. You might feel stuck, paralysed, numb, low, disconnected or fatigued.

LIMBIC SYSTEM Often called the 'emotional centre' of the brain, the main functions of the limbic system are emotional and memory regulation and processing, stimulation and learning and driving our threat/stress response.

PARASYMPATHETIC NERVOUS SYSTEM This branch of your nervous system slows things, and conserves energy and helps to calm down and shut off the sympathetic nervous system when it has been activated.

PROPRIOCEPTION/PROPRIOCEPTIVE INPUT Your ability to know where your body is in space. This sensory input (often through pressure to muscles/joints) informs the brain about our body's position and is often calm and regulating.

REGULATION Refers to feeling in control of your emotions, behaviours and thoughts and refers to a ventral vagal state.

SOMATIC 'Soma' is the Ancient Greek word for body. It is through body-based/somatic practices that we can regulate the nervous system, process emotions and trauma, rewire old reflexive patterns and build our resilience.

SYMPATHETIC NERVOUS SYSTEM Your sympathetic nervous system is all about activation and mobilisation. It is also responsible for your threat responses: fight and flight, feelings of anger, rage and irritability or of anxiety, worry, stress and panic. This is a state of hyperarousal. When in this activated state your adrenal glands will produce cortisol and adrenaline to prepare you to face a stressor. You may notice a faster heart rate, increased breath rate, slowed digestion, muscle tension, hypervigilance or brain fog.

❀ *THREAT RESPONSE* A threat response refers to your nervous system's fight, flight, freeze or fawn states (briefly: fight = movement towards; anger, flight = movement away; anxiety/panic, freeze = shutdown/ collapse, fawn = people pleasing). These are all unconscious responses in order to keep you safe when you face a stressor.

❀ *UP REGULATE* Bringing energy and movement into a nervous system that is hypoaroused/in a dorsal vagal response. It helps to bring balance when you feel down, stuck, unmotivated or dissociated.

❀ *VAGUS NERVE* The vagus nerve is one of the most important nerves in the body. It 'wanders' from the base of your brainstem and innervates most of your organs, including the heart, stomach and lungs. It's a two-way communication system, sending information from your organs to your brain and vice versa. It regulates internal functions like digestion, heart rate and respiratory rate. Your vagus nerve is intimately involved with your autonomic nervous system and threat responses and is the brake that helps engage your parasympathetic nervous system to regulate you in times of stress. This nerve can be blocked or damaged. It can develop 'low tone' from years of stress or trauma, which means it doesn't work effectively, causing unwanted effects on the body and mind like digestive issues, brain fog, anxiety, depression, low motivation, chronic pain and more. There are many ways to activate and increase your vagal tone.

❀ *VENTRAL VAGAL* One of two branches of your parasympathetic nervous system, the ventral vagal refers to the state when you feel calm, safe, curious, creative, compassionate, present, oriented to your environment and relaxed. This is also called 'rest, digest and restore' or 'tend and befriend'. When you are in a ventral vagal state your body will also be digesting food, sleeping well and feeling open to socialising and connecting with others.